CU00592107

101

GREAT ESCAPES

101
GREAT ESCAPES

Publisher: Polly Manguel
Project Editor: Gary Almond
Designer: Ron Callow/Design 23
Production Manager: Neil Randles

This edition first published in Great Britain in 2011 by
Bounty Books, a division of Octopus Publishing Group Limited
Endeavour House, 189 Shaftesbury Avenue,
London WC2H 8JY
www.octopusbooks.co.uk

An Hachette UK Company
www.hachette.co.uk

Copyright © 2011 Octopus Publishing Group Limited

All rights reserved. No part of this publication may be
reproduced, stored in a retrieval system, or transmitted, in
any form or by any means, electronic, mechanical,
photocopying, recording or otherwise without the prior
written permission of the publisher.

Text previously appeared in:
501 Must-Visit Destinations
501 Must-Be-There Events
501 Must-Visit Natural Wonders
501 Must-Visit Islands
501 Must-Take Journeys
501 Must-Visit Wild Places

A CIP catalogue record is available from the British Library

ISBN: 978-0-753721-99-5

Printed and bound in China

Please note:

We now know that political situations arise very quickly and a city or country that
was quite safe a short time ago can suddenly become a 'no-go' area. Please
check with the relevant authorities before booking tickets and travelling if you
think there could be a problem.

The seasons given in this book relate to the relevant hemisphere. Be sure to
check that you visit at the correct time.

Contents

Introduction

In the current age of low-cost airlines, all-inclusive resorts, tour parties and tacky souvenirs the world it seems is a smaller, more homogenized place, and the opportunities to escape your day-to-day life on a truly original break have become fewer and farther between.

This book is a guide for the more imaginative tourist. It details trips, destinations and events to help you escape not only your normal routine, but also the well-trodden, hackneyed getaways everyone has been on.

To best suit people's diverse tastes and interests *101 Great Escapes* is divided into a number of various categories. In 'Action & Adventure Escapes', it is the activity that distinguishes the break from the mainstream, be it cycling across the US, bridge jumping in Croatia or rafting in South Africa. The 'Rest & Relaxation Escapes' often involve doing nothing more than lying back and chilling out, but in areas of the world you may not immediately think of – and maybe won't be familiar with – allowing you to spend time away from the hustle and bustle of the modern world. Aboard a paddle steamer in Australia or sampling whisky in Scotland, your days will be completely free of stress or worry, making it almost impossible not to enjoy yourself. 'Off the Beaten Track Escapes' includes some of the most remote places on

earth, but also reveals undiscovered gems a stone's throw from commercial tourism spots. From the northern coast of Sweden to the southern tip of Argentina, travelling the heartland of Spain or Jordan's desert landscapes, the challenges of the journeys in this section are as fundamental as the destinations. Escape doesn't necessarily mean isolation – a passionate crowd, local ceremony or traditional celebration can provide an holistic retreat, and 'Experience Escapes' are intoxicating events or locations as far removed from your normal life as possible. A local football match in Argentina, a colourful harvest festival in India or the retro stylings of Cuba present sensory escapes, with often unfamiliar sights, sounds and smells. Finally, 'Alternative Escapes' suggests hidden treasures that wouldn't immediately spring to mind when booking a trip. These include carnival spent in Colombia, the barrier reef in Belize, exploring Norway on a postal liner – less commercial, more unspoilt destinations that remain blissfully free of coach-trips and snap-happy travellers do still exist; you just need to know where to look.

Everybody needs a little adventure in their life, providing a respite from routine. By escaping the ordinary and avoiding the mundane you will allow yourself to fully escape, whether for a few hours, days, weeks or months … and once you do, you'll never look back.

ACTION & ADVENTURE
ESCAPES

Ekstremsportveko

WHEN:
Late June
WHERE:
Voss
BEST FOR:
Sport and music
YOU SHOULD KNOW:
Athletes from Voss itself
have represented Norway at
every Winter Olympic
Games since 1948, except in
1972, and between them
have won six gold, five silver
and seven bronze medals.

Ekstremsportveko is the largest extreme sport and
music festival there is, and takes place each year in
western Norway. During the past 15 or 20 years, as our
personal freedom has become ever more confined by
health and safety laws, hygiene laws and more, it is
interesting to note that young people have become
exponentially more interested in extreme and
dangerous sports. Nowadays, it seems that those who
are driven to school when they could easily walk and
are forbidden to climb trees for fear of falling, are drawn
towards the undisputed adrenaline highs of mountain
climbing, paragliding, kite surfing and base jumping.

Voss, in western Norway, is perfectly positioned. It
lies on a beautiful lake and is surrounded by snow-
topped peaks, fast and furious white-water rivers and
thick forest. For some years it has been a centre for
adventure sports and in 1998 began to host the
extreme-sports week. Today over 1,000 competitors
from some 30 countries, as well as more than 20,000
spectators, arrive here each year. The festival is not just
for serious athletes, however: there are beginner
sessions for many of the sports, where you can learn the
basics from experts. For those with no desire to risk
their lives or limbs, a vicarious thrill can be had just
from watching others participate.

Try not to tire yourself out during the daytime – the
night life in Voss is almost as spectacular as the sporting
events. Apart from visiting the bars and restaurants –
where the local speciality is *smalahove*, a sheep's head
complete with eyes and tongue – a large festival tent is
set up for the duration and you can dance until you
drop to one of the many bands that come to play here
during festival week.

*PREVIOUS: A female
base jumper takes flight.*

*The parachute
swooping competition*

*Two extreme sports base
jumpers*

Chamonix-Zermatt Haute Route

Why go on foot or skis when there's a car or public transport available? Actually, if the journey rather than the destination is the thing it makes perfect sense to give a simple answer – 'because I can'. In the case of the Chamonix-Zermatt Haute Route, that reply really means something – this is one of Europe's ultimate physical challenges, and anyone who successfully undertakes this 180-km (110-mi) traverse through the Alps from Chamonix to Zermatt (bridging the spectacular gap between those two iconic Alpine mountains, Mont Blanc and the Matterhorn) can feel proud indeed – around half fail, especially in winter.

The summer walking route, pioneered by 19th-century English mountaineers, crosses Alpine meadows, passes shining lakes, skirts glaciers, goes through forests and visits picturesque mountain villages. There are variations allowing for a personal itinerary. In the case of a summer hike, the basic choice is between the original 'high' route and a lower-level option that avoids collapsing glaciers that have made the high route even more difficult. Along the original route hikers mostly stay at mountain huts, whilst the lower route involves staying in village accommodation.

The winter route, first skied in 1911, is one of the world's most prestigious ski tours, making a tortuous way through the highest and most dramatic Alpine scenery with skiers staying at high huts that allow them to cover considerable distances each day. To carry off this hazardous enterprise, both snow conditions and weather need to be favourable and again there are route decisions to be made, with a number of established variations to choose from. Whatever the route, the rewards are exhilarating skiing amidst breathtaking scenery.

Be warned – the Haute Route is arduous and should only be attempted by parties of superfit, highly experienced and well-prepared adventurers.

HOW:
On foot or on skis
WHEN TO GO:
Any time of year
TIME IT TAKES:
No less than 12 days on foot and a week on skis
HIGHLIGHTS:
Spectacular views all the way to the Matterhorn from the top of Col Superior du Tour at a dizzy altitude of 3,288 m (10,787 ft).
A welcome break at Champex-Lac, surrounded by woods and with a beautiful lake.
A worthwhile short-cut by cable car from Le Chable up the mountain to Verbier – incredible views as you relax.
Above the impressively sited Vignettes Hut – the best Alpine views you'll ever see from the Haute Route's high point at the 3,796-m (12,454-ft) Pigne d'Arolla summit.
YOU SHOULD KNOW:
Even in high summer the walking route is likely to involve crossing patches of snow, using crampons.

NEXT: A hiker heading towards the Matterhorn.

LEFT: Ski tourers on the Haute Route

13

Three Rivers Ride

HOW:
On horseback
WHEN TO GO:
May to September for the best weather
TIME IT TAKES:
At least a week for the full Ride – more if undertaking side exploration
HIGHLIGHTS:
A bottle of locally brewed farm cider from one of the village shops in Herefordshire – rather stronger than most commercial brews!
Cefn Hill near Hay-on-Wye – for wonderful views of England to one side and of Wales to the other
YOU SHOULD KNOW:
There is a further riding trail at either end of the Three Rivers Ride – the Sabrina Way in England and the Epynt Way in Wales.

This is part of Britain's National Bridle Network, a series of cross-country routes that is being developed for long-distance horse riders. The way-marked 153-km (95-mi) Three Rivers Ride through the glorious Welsh Marches starts at Tidbach near Bromyard in Worcestershire, enters Herefordshire at Wolferlow and crosses the Rivers Lugg and Wye before entering Wales at Hay Bluff and continuing through the Brecon Beacons National Park to the third and final river – the Usk – finally finishing at the Mountain Centre (Brecon Beacons Visitor Centre) near the town of Brecon.

This really is a scenic ride par excellence, with stunning views all the way. It is a journey of two halves. The first section in offers a peaceful ride past cider orchards and through classic English countryside, across the rapidly flowing River Lugg and along the breathtaking Wye Valley. After crossing the Welsh border the second section runs through a sweeping bank of hills, along the Western flank of the Black Mountains, skirting the picturesque Llangors Lake and crossing the River Usk.

Some riders do the full journey, whilst others prefer to concentrate on the more dramatic mountain scenery of the 56-km (35-mi) Welsh section. The

weather in the Brecon Beacons can be unpredictable, and the Path itself is often far from human habitation, so riders are advised to take appropriate all-weather gear and be sure to tell someone their plans before starting out for the day. Don't assume you can rely on a mobile phone to summon assistance if something goes wrong in the remote Welsh hills – there is rarely a signal.

Those who don't have their own horse will find several riding and trekking stables who can provide mounts for the Three Rivers Ride – including sturdy and locally bred Welsh cobs. A selection of bed and breakfast stops for both rider and horse can be found along the route, together with self-catering cottages that have stables.

Mist hanging over Brecon Beacons National Park.

A mozo, or runner, is gored by a bull.

Pamplona

WHAT IS THERE TO SEE:
The Museo de Navarra, the
citadel, the cathedral.
WHEN TO GO:
The festival runs from 6–14
July.
YOU SHOULD KNOW:
Every year there are serious
injuries sustained in the
encierro.

Pamplona has been the capital of Navarre (Navarra)
in northern Spain since the ninth century and is
believed to have been originally founded by the
Roman general, Pompey.

Ernest Hemingway put Pamplona and its 'fiesta'
firmly on the map when he published his book *The
Sun Also Rises*. At midday on 6 July the fiesta gets
going with a bang as a rocket explodes outside the

town hall, and the crowd tie their red handkerchiefs around their necks, singing and shouting '*Viva San Fermín!*' On the last night, 14 July, the party comes to an end with crowds of people holding candles and singing Basque songs in the main square.

The eight-day fiesta of San Fermín is a week of non-stop riotous parties, fireworks, parades, music, dancing and, at 8.00 am each day, the *encierro* (running of the bulls). Six bulls are released to run through the old town's cobbled streets, on their way to the bull-ring for the evening's bull-fight. Every day, too, men take the opportunity to run through the streets with the bulls, risking serious injury, even death.

If this sounds too dangerous for you, Pamplona also has Spain's best medieval military architecture in the form of the star-shaped citadel and city walls that Philip II had built in order to defend against the depredations of the French.

NEXT: Crowds watch from high vantage points to see the chaos.

19

Bridge Jumping at Mostar

WHEN:
July, but check with the Tourist Board
WHERE:
Stari Most Bridge, Mostar
BEST FOR:
Local tradition – young men have been jumping from this bridge for centuries – and extreme sport.
YOU SHOULD KNOW:
This feat must be taken very seriously. It is extremely easy to get hurt. The local lads are very territorial about their bridge – pay up if you want to have a go.

The historic town of Mostar is enchantingly situated in a green valley surrounded by hills covered with deciduous trees, mountains rising in the distance. Mostar's famous Stari Most bridge, built in 1567 to boost trade between Turkey and Europe, towers above the greenish-blue waters of the River Neretva as it runs through the centre of town. Historically, on July 31 each year, local men competed in diving from the bridge into the chilly waters beneath. Today, the interest in extreme sports brings people from many different countries to try their luck here.

Mostar's history is long, complex and, recently, tragic; it suffered appallingly during the Balkan civil war of the 1990s, when it was bombed, shelled and laid siege to by both Bosnian Serbs and the Croats. Much of

the town was razed, including Stari Most, and the scars of war are still visible. Today, in a spirit of reconciliation, Mostar is governed by both Croats and Bosnian Muslims, and a huge reconstruction project is ongoing. Psychologically, its most important work was the rebuilding, stone for stone, of Stari Most. Partially funded by UNESCO, it is now listed as a World Heritage Site.

Protected at each end by fortified towers, the bridge stands some 21 m (70 ft) above the river – an Olympic high-diving platform is a mere 10 m (33 ft). During the summer, many young men earn themselves extra money by collecting payment from passing tourists. When a small crowd has gathered, off they leap, usually feet first. At the diving competition, however, the river banks are crowded with locals and tourists alike. All watch with their hearts in their mouths as more and more perfectly executed dives, including somersaults and backflips, are performed to wild cheers and applause.

A local jumper takes the plunge.

The new 'Old Bridge'

Haraz Mountain Trek

HOW:
On foot
WHEN TO GO:
April, May, September and October
TIME IT TAKES:
Three days plus
HIGHLIGHTS:
The breathtaking, peaceful countryside, and the uncommercialized villages

The Haraz Mountains, west of Sana'a, is an area of steep hillsides, high peaks and lovely stone villages. From the 12th century, the mountains served as refuge for descendents of the Ismaili Sulayhids, and many of the villages date from this period. During Ottoman occupation this was a strategic area where cannons guarded mountain passes. Farming is intensive – even the steepest slopes have been terraced, and monsoon rain is gathered for irrigation. A large proportion of Yemen's scarce arable land lies in these mountains and a wide variety of crops are grown.

Trekking in Yemen is not organized, with no maps or

Terraced farming around Manakha

Al Hajjara village

marked trails, but the Manakha area is perfect for
day-treks. Two of the villages, Manakha and Al
Hajjara, have facilities for visitors and make good
bases. Hostel accommodation offers packed lunches
and evening entertainment of local music and dance,
and can arrange guides and camping equipment for
longer treks. Manakha is the market town for the
surrounding region; Al Hajjara, to the west, is a lovely
fortified hilltop village.

There are many enjoyable circular day-walks using
the network of paths between villages – south to Al-
Khutayb, an Ismaili pilgrimage site, west to Jabal
Masar and a scattering of historic hamlets, or Jabal
Shibam, the highest peak in the region. Longer treks
to the edge of the mountains, where peaceful villages
look down over steep escarpments, or north and
south out of the Manakha region can be organized.
Guides will arrange camping outside villages.

YOU SHOULD KNOW:
Most of the villages in the
Haraz lie at around 2,000 m
(6,500 ft) – climbing even
the higher peaks (just under
3,000 m/9,750 ft) is fairly
straightforward.
Sudden bursts of heavy rain
can reduce temperatures
and send large boulders
rolling down the slopes.

25

The Pamir Highway

HOW:
By 4x4 or bike
WHEN TO GO:
July to September
TIME IT TAKES:
Five to seven days by 4x4,
three weeks by mountain
bike
HIGHLIGHTS:
Yamchun – 12th century fort
with spectacular view.
Bathing in the Garm-
Chashma and Bibi Fatima
hot springs.
Lake Karak-Kul – salt lake
formed by meteorite impact
millions of years ago.
Views from the Ak-Baital
Pass, 4,655 m (15,270 ft).
YOU SHOULD KNOW:
This is a demanding journey
whether you travel by jeep
or bike. You will be travelling
at very high altitudes so
must be physically fit. You
can shorten the journey by
taking a plane part of the
way, from Dushanbe to
Khorugh – a spectacular
scenic flight through the
mountains that is an
experience in itself.

The Pamir Highway is one of the highest, most thrilling, least-travelled routes in the world. Here, at the meeting point of the Tien Shan, Hindu Kush and Karakoram mountain ranges, is some of the most extraordinary and beautiful terrain on the planet, an eerie empty land of parched ochre rock, hot springs and turquoise glacial lakes set amongst the magnificent snow-capped peaks of the world's highest mountains.

Built by the Russians as a Soviet supply road, the Highway runs for some 1,250 km (780 mi) from Dushanbe to Osh along an ancient Silk Road route across the Pamir Plateau. Subject to erosion, earthquakes and landslides, the road is in a constant state of disrepair, making for a journey full of sudden unforeseen hazards. There is almost no traffic and, apart from shepherds herding their flocks, scarcely a soul to be seen. You will, however, stumble upon plenty of monuments – petroglyphs, ancient temples, Buddhist stupas and ruined fortresses, charting several millennia of history.

The Highway runs eastwards from Dushanbe across the plains, winding steeply upwards through rugged mountains to Khalaikum. You pass rusting hulks of abandoned Russian tanks and lurid signs warning of minefields as you manoeuvre your way through old

landslips and uncontained streams sloshing across the
road. The air grows colder and howling winds blow
through an increasingly desolate landscape as you
climb over the Koi-Tezek Pass at 4,200 m (13,775 ft)
and set out across the Pamir Plateau towards China.
At the frontier, the road turns northwards along the
Chinese border up to Ak-Baital Pass at 4,655 m
(15,270 ft) before descending to the hauntingly
beautiful Lake Kara-Kul, through the lush pastures
and dramatic gorges of the Alai Valley in Kyrgyzstan,
to end this epic road trip at the colourful city of Osh.

*A motorcyclist on the
Pamir Highway*

*NEXT: The Highway
passes through stunning
scenery.*

Orkhon Valley

HOW:
On horseback
WHEN TO GO:
May to October
TIME IT TAKES:
Ten days
HIGHLIGHTS:
Galloping across the steppe.
Staying in a traditional *ger* camp.
Ruins of Kharkhorum –
Ghengis Khan's capital.
Erdene Zuu Monastery –
most ancient Buddhist monastery in Mongolia

Mongolia is the most sparsely populated country in the world, a vast untamed expanse of mountain, forest, desert and plateau. In this nomadic land where more than thirty per cent of the population are still herdsmen and there are scarcely any roads, riding is the normal means of getting around. Mongolians have an almost symbiotic relationship with their horses – calm, surefooted ponies that easily handle the rough terrain unshod.

An expedition by horse to the Valley will open your eyes to a way of life that is utterly unfamiliar. The

Orkhon is the cradle of Central Asian nomadic societies, a World Heritage Cultural Landscape where the inhabitants live in harmony with nature, continuing pastoral traditions and shamanic religious practices that are unchanged for some two millenia.

As you ride through the wildflower pastures by the River Orkhon, the only signs of human life are the scattered *gers* (yurt tents) of nomad families. A camping trek of some 200 km (125 mi) along the river valley and up into the Khangai Mountains, through verdant, volcanic plains and forested gorges to the dramatic cascade of the Orkhon waterfall is a liberating escape from the complexities of the post-modern age. Here there is just you, your horse and

Yurts in the Orkhon Valley

YOU SHOULD KNOW:
You should be a reasonably competent horse rider to go on this trek. Alternative means of transport are yak cart, mountain bike or 4x4.

nature in her rawest form.

Incredible as it may seem, you are travelling through the heart of the largest empire in the history of the world. At its height in the 13th century, the Mongol Empire stretched across Central Asia from Beijing to the borders of Hungary. Ghengis Khan held sway over more than a 100 million people from his capital city of Kharkhorum in the Orkhon Valley. The remnants can be seen today – ruins standing as testaments that this remote valley was once the centre of the world.

Horses graze by the Orkhon River.

Rafting Nine Bends River

Wuyi Shan, in northern Fujian province, is southeast China's most remote mountain region. Its incomparable scenic beauty was recognized 4,000 years ago by the Yue people, and it became a site of pilgrimage for Taoism, Buddhism and Confucianism. Already a protected area for 1,500 years before gaining the UNESCO grand slam of World Biosphere and World Natural, Cultural and Historical Heritage Site, Wuyi is the ultimate Chinese expression of the potential for harmony between nature and man. Its heart-stirring landscapes are littered with the temples, palaces and pavilions created in tribute to the aesthetics of Confucian philosophy, whose greatest spear-carrier, the 10th century neo-Confucian Zhu Xi, lived and taught here for fifty years.

Jiuqu (Nine Bends) Gorge, a 10-km (6-mi) section of the 63-km (39-mi) Jiuqu River, is the geographical heart of this summation of Chinese history and

HOW:
On a raft
WHEN TO GO:
Year-round
TIME IT TAKES:
1.5-2 hours (Xingcun – Wuyi Town, through the Nine Bends); one to two days (starting further upriver enables you to reflect in peace on the extent of the region's natural beauty, and renders you immune to the noisy crowds of rafters along the Nine Bends stretch when you get there).

The view of the river from Mount Wuyi

33

River rafting at Tianyou Feng.

HIGHLIGHTS:
The Palace complex and other Minyue remains at Xingcun – the most extensive and best preserved of all South China's Han Dynasty sites, over 2,000 years old.
The Wuyi Nature Reserve (of which the Nine Bends is part) – 95 per cent intact sub-tropical forest.
The 'fairy boats' – the boat-coffins dating back 4,000 years, stuffed into caves and fissures all along the soaring rock walls of the gorge.
YOU SHOULD KNOW:
You can save a lot of time and anxiety at the raft pier by prebooking through a tour agent.

culture – and the water element in the formula for harmony. So when you raft the Jiuqu Gorge, you embrace a welter of Chinese philosophy which dictates significance in every rock, every mist of spray, the towering cliffs and solitary, jungle-topped stacks wreathed in cloud; and in the deep placid green pools, the wind-dashed waterfalls and squabbling, rock-strewn rapids of the watercourse. The rafting itself needs no crash-helmet commando training: you sit on bamboo chairs set on six, lashed-together bamboo poles, and swirl gently down stream.

It really is worth reading about Wuyi before you raft the Nine Bends. Each bend reveals a new set of surprises, a geography saturated with sophisticated meaning: with just an inkling of the nature of the reverence in which the Nine Bends are held, you get a four-dimensional view of what are otherwise merely world-class panoramas. On the water, with visual stimuli at maximum pleasure, this is one of the few places you can go 'holistic' rafting.

Selous Game Reserve

Selous Game Reserve is an absolutely enormous area of some 50,000 sq km (19,300 sq mi). Large enough to be a country in its own right, it occupies five per cent of Tanzania, and is larger than Switzerland. Inscribed as a UNESCO World Heritage Site in 1982, sections of the reserve were first designated as a hunting area in 1905, and in 1922, when extra land was added, it was named after Fredrick Selous, a popular Victorian explorer and author. Constant additions to its boundaries have made it one of the largest game reserves in the world.

The landscape consists of rolling, grassy woodland and plains covered by unusually lush grass and tangled vegetation as well as the Rufiji River and its

WHAT IS IT:
The second largest game reserve in Africa, home to a unique combination of both East and South African wildlife.

HOW TO GET THERE:
Most visitors fly into Selous from Dar es Salaam; road travel is only possible during the dry season.

An elephant peeks around a tree.

WHEN TO GO:
June to November for
viewing game along the
rivers and January to April
for bird watching.
NEAREST TOWN:
Dar es Salaam 150 km
(94 mi)
DON'T MISS:
Stiegler's Gorge, boating
safaris, walking safaris
YOU SHOULD KNOW:
This is a region of malarial
mosquitos and Tsetse flies.

36

delta. This impressive river is the life blood of Selous,
from narrow, rock-sided Stiegler's Gorge to the
tributaries, sand rivers, oxbow lakes, lagoons and
channels of the delta, it is the main water source of
the region.

Best known for its huge herds of elephants, which
migrate annually across the border to Niassa Game
Reserve in Mozambique, the park is home to large
numbers of animals. Lions, leopards and cheetahs all
thrive here, hunting antelope, wildebeest, eland and
zebra. One third of all the remaining endangered
African wild dogs roam freely and thrive in Selous,

*A gang of four
Maasai Giraffe*

which also contains some of the region's last black
rhinos. The river is home to hippos and crocodiles,
and attracts many of the reserve's 440 species of bird.

Selous has various safari camps and lodges, mainly
situated around the Gorge area, but is otherwise
uninhabited. Roads here are impassable during the
rainy season, but camps can be reached by plane.
Safaris by boat are increasingly popular, and it is one
of the only African reserves that allow safaris on foot,
accompanied by an armed ranger. Few visitors come
here, but those who do enter an absolutely untamed
wilderness and gain a life-enhancing experience.

Bwindi Impenetrable National Park

WHAT IS IT:
True African jungle – one of east Africa's largest forests; home to over a third of the world's population of Mountain gorillas.
HOW TO GET THERE:
By road from Kampala via Kabale
WHEN TO GO:
December to February and May to August
NEAREST TOWN:
Kabale 29 km (18 mi)
DON'T MISS:
The many spectacular birds and butterflies
YOU SHOULD KNOW:
In many places the forest is indeed impenetrable; only 12 visitor permits are issued per day.

Bwindi Impenetrable National Park is, at 331 sq km (128 sq mi), one of the largest areas of tropical rainforest in east Africa. Situated in a landscape of steep, rugged hills and deep, narrow valleys along the border with the Democratic Republic of Congo, it warrants its name. This is a prime example of the jungle of our imagination – vast trees, draped with creepers, mistletoe and orchids, struggle to reach the sunlight, while beneath them the dense undergrowth of twisting vines and ferns occasionally gives way to

thickets of bamboo, swamps, marshes, rivers and grassland. Where the sun breaks through the leafy canopy, exotic and colourful plants such as heliconia add sudden splashes of colour.

The flora and fauna in Bwindi are incredibly impressive, with over 200 types of tree and 100 species of fern. At least 120 species of mammal live here, and the area is rich with primates – Colobus monkeys leap between branches, families of chimpanzees search for fruit, vervets and baboons chatter and hoot, adding a subtext to the twittering and screeching of some 350 different species of bird.

Amongst Bwindi's populations of endangered species are some 23 families of Mountain gorilla.

The Impenetrable Forest is aptly named - dense foliage protects its inhabitants.

Twenty three families of gorilla inhabit the area.

Living at a lower altitude than those in the Virunga Mountains, it is thought that these may be a distinct subspecies, with shorter hair and longer limbs. Four of the families are used to humans and can be tracked and observed, but there are other fascinating safaris and hiking trails here too – even on the shortest stretch you are likely to see primates, duikers and both forest and grassland birds as well as some of the glorious 202 types of butterfly. Stand in the jungle and wonder at the silence as you watch the cream-banded swallowtail, which occurs only here, flutter past, then enjoy the sudden sounds of monkeys and birds exploding into action for a few minutes before stillness and tranquillity reign again.

Running the Orange River

For those in search of adventure, running the Orange River in the Richtersveldt National Park on the border of South Africa and Namibia is just the ticket. In this isolated part of the Northern Cape, the Orange River's long journey from the Drakensberg range to the Atlantic Ocean finally ends. Here, this majestic river is a long, green-fringed oasis that offers scenic stretches of serene water as it twists and turns through a striking desert landscape, with occasional fun rapids to spice up the journey.

This is a river run to be undertaken with a guide, either solo or with a group. The Orange River is usually tackled using two-person inflatable rafts, kayaks or canoes, sometimes with the support of a larger raft carrying supplies. A typical trip will be around 80-km (50-mi) long and different guides and organizers use various starting and take-out points. There is usually a base camp at the start where personal belongings may be left, with transport back at the end of the trip. Most expeditions assemble at

HOW:
By raft, kayak or canoe
WHEN TO GO:
March to January
TIME IT TAKES:
Four to six days for a typical journey
HIGHLIGHTS:
Rapids like Dead Man's Rapid and Sjambok Rapid – not too dangerous, but definitely enough to get the blood pounding.
Birds – the water and banks are alive with species including cormorants, goliath herons, fish eagles and kingfishers.

Canoes pulled up on the bank as the sun sets.

Sand dunes along the banks at Richtersveld

Vioolsdrift on the Namibian border, just upriver from the Park – and some 350 km (217 mi) from the mouth of the Orange River – from where paddlers are driven to base camp.

The Richtersveldt National Park has recently been made a UNESCO World Heritage Site and it's easy to understand why. The Richtersveldt is one of the most remote and unspoiled areas of South Africa, and one of the best ways to see this barren but extraordinary place is from the river that runs through it – some say the best way. It's a true wilderness experience, in a rocky landscape that one writer has eloquently called 'too beautiful to describe'. Somehow, that says it all – though that means you must see for yourself!

Nahanni River on a raft

A Nahanni rafting expedition is truly a trip of a lifetime. Over the course of this 94 km (150 mi) journey from Virginia Falls to Blackstone Landing, this fast-flowing river drops a heart pumping 396 m (1,300 ft). Each section of this epic voyage takes you through canyons, over rapids and past some of the most stunning scenery on Earth.

Even the names conjure up images of danger and excitement as you tumble through Hell's Gate, pass Headless Creek and camp out in Deadmen Valley. So remote is this region of north-western Canada that the only practical way to arrive is by air. This start to the voyage could not be more spectacular, as you land alongside the towering Virginia Falls.

Fed by the melt waters of the Mackenzie Mountains, the Nahanni River provides the rafter with the most thrilling of rides. From the figure-of-eight rapids of Hell's Gate to the giant waves of George's Riffle, this is a true test of oars, people and raft. The welcome respite of overnight camping could not be in more imposing surroundings, and the 1,200 m (3,900 ft) walls of Third Canyon are the most magnificent of sights to wake up to in the morning.

The rushing noise of the river is constant and reminds you of the challenges that lie ahead. Towards the end of this epic voyage you pass, as if by design, Kraus' Hotsprings where you can soothe your aching limbs, rejoice in nature and congratulate yourself on nearly completing this most exhilarating of journeys. It is then just a short paddle along the braided channels of The Splits where the river finally loses some of its rage.

HOW:
By raft
DEPART:
Virginia Falls, NWT
WHEN TO GO:
June to August, when the ice has melted.
TIME IT TAKES:
About one week
HIGHLIGHTS:
Virginia Falls – difficult to tear oneself away.
The thrilling run through Painted Canyon.
The view of Tlogotsho Plateau from Deadmen Valley.
The lush steep-sided forest as you near Blackstone Landing.
YOU SHOULD KNOW:
The beauty of rafting is that even a relative beginner can tackle the hardest of runs if accompanied by experienced people. You do have to be fit however, as there is a lot of equipment to be carried on trips such as these.

NEXT: Virginia Falls, in Nahanni National Park Reserve, are twice as high as Niagra Falls.

The East Coast Trail

The 540 km (337 mi) East Coast Trail hugs the scenic shores of the Avalon Peninsula of Newfoundland and Labrador. This grand trail is very much a work in progress, with 220 km (138 mi) of the trail well marked. The remainder of it is accessible but not signposted and provides a greater challenge to the more experienced hiker.

The marked section of the Trail stretches from Fort Amherst, in historic St John's, to Cappahayden, on the beautiful southern shore. It is equipped with trail signage, maps and supporting information to enhance your hiking experience along the coast and through the wilderness. It consists of a series of 18 paths each with a northern and a southern trailhead. Each of these paths can be hiked individually, some are easy strolls, whilst others are longer and more demanding.

As is fitting for a trail of this magnitude there is much to see and explore. This system of what were once backcountry routes and hunting trails takes the hiker through provincial parks, national historic sites and ecological reserves. Sustenance and rest can be taken at any one of the charming fishing villages that line the route.

There are currently plans by the volunteer East Coast Trail Association to expand the marked route to Trepassey in the south and Topsoil in the north. The Association should be your first port of call when attempting this epic trail as their encyclopaedic knowledge of the area can prove invaluable to even the most seasoned of hikers.

HOW:
On foot
DEPART:
Fort Amherst, NL
WHEN TO GO:
More navigable from May to October
TIME IT TAKES:
Allow a month to complete the whole trail
HIGHLIGHTS:
The Spout (a wave-driven geyser)
The National Historic Sites of Cape Spear, Signal Hill, and Cape Race
The suspension bridge at the historic abandoned community of La Manche
YOU SHOULD KNOW:
The trail is left intentionally unpaved and unspoiled. This means that underfoot conditions can be slippery and several of the walks are close to cliff edges. Therefore, hiking the trail has an inherently greater risk than taking a stroll in an urban park.

NEXT: Fort Amherst, St John's, Newfoundland

Trans-Canada Train Journey

There is no rule which states that crossing a whole continent will ever be easy and this journey certainly tests the mettle of the traveller. Nevertheless, the sights you see and the people you meet on this epic trip will stay in the memory for the rest of your life. Nearly all those who make the journey from Halifax to Vancouver do so for fun (flying is cheaper and quicker) – and this gives the whole experience a real party feel.

Completing the journey currently comprises three stages. The first, from Halifax to Montreal, takes you from the extremely picturesque Nova Scotia coast, through New Brunswick. Skirting the Appalachian Mountains, you are then transported to Montreal, the beating heart of French Canada. The second leg allows you to sample the most modern railway Canada has to offer. The Montreal to Toronto link feels strangely normal compared with the rest of the trip. Business people barely look up from their laptops as

HOW:
By train
DEPART:
Halifax, NS
WHEN TO GO:
Year round, but schedules can be disrupted in winter (November to April).
TIME IT TAKES:
Currently it takes about six days with a long stopover in either Montreal or Toronto. If you want to see a lot of Canada allow two weeks and spend time in Montreal, Toronto, Jasper and Vancouver.

The city of Montreal lies on the shore of the St Lawrence River.

HIGHLIGHTS:
Old Montreal – fabulous, French and funky.
Mount Robson and Pyramid Falls – in the Rockies.
Vancouver – it really is as good as they say: the sea, mountains, excellent affordable eating and really friendly people.

the train passes along the St Lawrence River, past the Thousand Islands and along the shore of Lake Ontario.

From Toronto, Canada's most modern of cities, you embark on the truly monumental part of the train ride. The seemingly endless forests of Northern Ontario eventually give way to wide open prairies as you cross the Continent's interior – the vastness of it all is quite breathtaking. After two nights on board, the train approaches the Rockies. Waterfalls and sheer rock faces heave in to view one after another and this is the time to grab a seat in the panoramic dome car. After this, Kamloops is the last major stop before arriving in Vancouver and your chance to experience the city often voted the 'World's Best Place to Live'.

The Rockies - a panoramic dome allows for a 360 degree view.

The American Birkebeiner

The annual Birkebeiner cross-country ski race, known affectionately as the Birkie, is the largest event of its kind in North America. At 51 km (32 mi) long, it attracts some 8,000 skiers of varying ability and 20,000 spectators to a three-day marathon of events in Wisconsin, of which the Birkie and the shorter Kortelopet races are the climax.

The Birkie was founded in 1973, its name commemorating a famous event in Norway's history. In 1206, during the Norwegian civil war, a group of soldiers, known as Birkebeiners for their birch-bark protective leggings, smuggled the illegitimate 18-month-old son of King Sverresson from Lillehammer to the safety of Trondheim on skis, saving his life and enabling him to grow up and take the throne himself. Set in the glorious Chequamegon-Nicolet National Forest that covers much of northwest Wisconsin, the race starts in Cable and ends in Hayward, two towns with a combined population of less than 3,000. The race is the biggest date in the local calendar, as thousands of enthusiasts pour into the area from around the world.

Competitors set off in waves on a course that climbs and rolls to the high point of Firetower Hill, 120 m (400 ft) above the start point. From here there are many tricky descents and arduous climbs before crossing the frozen Lake Hayward into town, past thousands of cheering spectators lining the finishing point on Main Street. The Birkie is not just for professional athletes; it is for everyone who loves cross-country skiing. Some have raced it many times; others have never participated in a marathon ski journey in their lives. All who cross the finishing line not only feel a tremendous sense of achievement but

WHEN:
The last weekend in February
WHERE:
Northwest Wisconsin
BEST FOR:
Cross-country skiing through a pristine National Forest
YOU SHOULD KNOW:
The American Birkebeiner is one of the Worldloppet Ski Federation's worldwide cross-country ski marathons. At Norway's Birkebeinerrennet race, skiers traditionally carry backpacks weighing 3.5 kg (7.5 lb).

Skiers cross the start line.

also receive a commemorative medallion to remind them of this beautiful course and the camaraderie of skiing through the forest with thousands of like-minded people.

Alexander Archipelago

Thayer Lake, Admiralty Island

You need lots of fingers to count the islands in the rugged Alexander Archipelago, which stretches for 485 km (200 mi), hugging the southeastern coast of Alaska – there are about 1,100 of them. They are the tops of submerged mountains rising steeply from the Pacific Ocean. Deep fjords and channels separate mainland and islands, which have inhospitable, irregular coasts. The whole area is densely forested with fir woods and temperate rain forests. Much of the archipelago is protected from development and teems with wildlife.

The main economic activities are tourism, fishing

WHEN TO GO:
Unless you want to risk being marooned, go between mid-May and mid-September.
HOW TO GET THERE:
Fly Alaska Airlines to the state capital of Juneau on the mainland, which offers a good ferry service to main islands. There are bush carriers who will undertake floatplane charters.

Bears at Warm Springs Bay on Baranof Island

HIGHLIGHTS:
The Pack Creek Brown Bear Viewing Area on Admiralty Island (permit required from the US Forest Service).
A scenic ride on Prince of Wales Island's Inter-Island ferry service.
Spectacular Glacier Bay National Park, with headquarters at Bartlett Cove, 105 km (65 m) from state capital Juneau (fly in to nearby Gustavus).

and logging. The largest islands are Admiralty, Baranof, Chichagof, Dall, Kupreanof, Revillagigedo, Prince of Wales and Wrangell. Alaska's period of Russian domination is reflected in the names of several islands and the archipelago itself, which is called after Alexander Baranof, who ran the Russian-American Fur Company in the early 19th century – or Tsar Alexander II, depending on who you listen to.

People are thinly scattered throughout this vast area, with the main centres of population being Ketchikan on Revillagigedo and Sitka on Baranov, each with some 8,000 souls – the latter was once the capital of Russian America. The archipelago is traversed by heavy boat traffic along the Inside Passage, a sheltered route that follows a path between the mainland and coastal islands of British Columbia and the Alaska Panhandle.

There's no point in pretending that Alaska is a conventional tourist destination. The Alexander Archipelago perfectly illustrates this, offering both the challenges and rewards that make a visit to the 49th state an unforgettable expedition. There is no road access, so the only ways in are by sea or air, but those who make the effort will be rewarded by the ultimate wilderness experience.

A Humpback Whale dives in Frederick Sound.

HOW:
By car or motorbike
DEPART:
Prudhoe Bay, AK
WHEN TO GO:
Start between May and
August, to travel the
Alaskan leg without risking
frostbite!
TIME IT TAKES:
How long have you got?
Allow at least four months
HIGHLIGHTS:
The Alamo in
San Antonio, TX.
Quito – the capital city of
Ecuador is a charming,
beautiful city that shows
urban South America at its
very best.
The Tierra del Fuego
National Park – not just
because it's journey's end,
but for the dramatic
scenery, waterfalls,
mountains, forests and
glaciers.

The Pan-American Highway

The world's longest drivable road is the Pan-American
Highway, a system with a total length of some 48,000
km (30,000 mi). It passes through Canada, the USA,
Mexico, Guatemala, El Salvador, Honduras, Nicaragua,
Costa Rica, Panama, Colombia, Ecuador, Peru, Chile
and Argentina. With various branches the whole
system adds up to a vast and rambling network.

The intrepid traveller must drive from Prudhoe Bay in Alaska down to the Panama Canal. Although the Pan-American Highway has no official status in the USA and Canada, the accepted route follows the Alaska Highway. After reaching Canada, the road splits at Edmonton, one route going via the Great Lakes, Minneapolis and Dallas, the other taking in Calgary, Denver and Albuquerque. The two meet at San Antonio in Texas, before reaching the 'official' Pan-American Highway at the Mexican border south of Monterrey.

Thereafter it runs through Central America via

The Centennial Bridge spans the Panama Canal.

YOU SHOULD KNOW:
It's not just the demanding terrain that will slow you down – there are 13 national borders to be crossed.

Mexico City and San Salvador to Panama City. There the road stops, briefly broken by the Darién Gap, a 90-km (55-mi) stretch of rain forest that may be crossed on foot, by bicycle, motorbike or ATV by reckless adventurers willing to brave bandits, swamps and jungle. Thereafter, the Highway resumes its often spectacular and sometimes dangerous journey, as the road follows the Pacific coast down through Cali, Quito, Antofagasta and Valparaiso, before cutting across to the Atlantic at Buenos Aires. That marks the official end of the Highway, but there are two unofficial branches – one continuing down the west coast from Valparaiso to Quellon, the other from Buenos Aires to Ushuaia at the tip of South America. This latter route is, of course, mandatory for anyone who wishes to be one of the few individuals on the planet to have travelled America from top to toe.

The Pan-American Highway in the Nazca Desert, Peru

Pico Duarte

*Riding burros on a
forest trail.*

Pico Duarte (3,087 m/10,128 ft)) is the highest
mountain in the Caribbean. More significantly, it is the
centrepiece of the huge Cordillera Central Reserve of
Bermúdez National Park, and almost untouched by
the kind of tourism that threatens to make a Disney
World of other parts of the Dominican Republic. The
Park is uninhabited, a pristine wilderness of clear
mountain rivers, jungle forests alive with the darting
colours of hummingbirds and parrots, and the most
magnificent landscapes in the Caribbean. Pico Duarte
itself is only one of several similar peaks, and
incorporates distinct sub-tropical eco-zones ranging
from coconut palms and swaying bamboo groves to
humid mountain forest, mountain rainforest and cool
alpine scrub and pine.

Of the five routes to Pico Duarte, all are strenuous
hikes of between 3 to 6 days and 46 to 108 km (28 to

HOW:
On foot
WHEN TO GO:
Year-round – but never
without a waterproof coat,
winter clothing, a sleeping
bag and hiking boots.
Traversing distinct climate
zones almost guarantees
unstable weather at any
time of year.
TIME IT TAKES:
3 days, 46 km (28 mi) round
trip (La Cienaga); 5 days, 90
km (56 mi) (Mata Grande); 6
days, 86 km (53 mi) (Los
Corralitos); 6 days, 96 km
(59 mi) (Sabaneta); 6 days,
108 km (67 mi) (Las
Lagunas).

57

The great view from Pico Duarte

HIGHLIGHTS:
Climbing the highest mountain in North America, east of the Mississippi. The variety and numbers of birds – including trogons, hispaniolan parrots, palm chats, red-tailed hawks, and zumbador hummingbirds. Riding mules (hire as many as you want: the rule of thumb is one guide and one mule for every five hikers).

YOU SHOULD KNOW:
With one or two extra mules, even small children can enjoy trekking on and around Pico Duarte. Some have been known to sleep happily while strapped to a mule on a 9-degree gradient.

67 mi). The most popular starts 25 km (13 mi) south west of Jarabacoa, from the village of La Cienaga where you have to register for the 46 km (28 mi) round trip, and hire a guide and mule (the mule is all but mandatory – if only as insurance for porterage and safety). Early in the morning, you follow the bubbling rivers up into the wild woodlands, serenaded by Mourning Doves. The dense forest thins, and gaps in the canopy reveal more and more of Hispaniola's fabled, translucent beauty. By nightfall you reach a ramshackle cabin called La Compartición, where the trails meet and hiking parties prepare for the pre-dawn scramble up the last 5 km (3 mi), through scented pines and open meadows, to greet the sunrise from the bare, rocky summit.

On a clear day with the clouds flushed pink below you, with the emerald forest and blue sea sharp contrasts in the distance, Pico Duarte's rugged antiquity fully justifies its mythic status in the Caribbean imagination. A magical trek.

Semuc Champey

Semuc Champey means 'sacred water' in Mayan and it certainly lives up to its name. It is quite unlike anything you have ever seen, in an idyllic mountain setting of tropical forest, full of wildlife, with radiantly coloured butterflies, hummingbirds and kingfishers darting around.

You make your way through the forest along the River Cahabon to meet an extraordinary sight – a series of small ponds and pools, 1-4 m (3-13 ft) deep, fed by the waterfalls and streams that run down the mountainsides. They are a scintillating range of colours, varying in intensity from pale turquoise to deep emerald and violet. Then you realize that the river is running below you and that these pools are set in the dented surface of a natural limestone bridge

WHAT IS IT:
A unique limestone formation
HOW TO GET THERE:
By road, 7 hours from Guatemala City and 3 hours from Coban
WHEN TO GO:
Less hot and humid in the dry season, November to April
NEAREST TOWN:
Lanquin 11 km (7 mi)
DON'T MISS:
The caves of Lanquin, with navigable streams, wildlife and pre-Hispanic artefacts.

One of the many limestone waterfalls

YOU SHOULD KNOW:
It is best to hire a guide to take you through the sometimes precipitous, heavily forested terrain. Tourists have died falling into the river and then being dragged down into the tunnel under the bridge.

that crosses the Cahabon River. It is an almost unbelievable sight and it is impossible not to be awestruck by its strange overwhelming beauty.

The torrential river beneath you spins wildly down, with a deafening noise as it is forcibly sucked into a limestone tunnel, only to re-emerge 350 m (1,150 ft) further on, where water from the top of the bridge cascades down in waterfalls to join it. It is a difficult

An aerial view reveals the limestone ridges.

spot to reach so it is worth spending one or two nights camping here. There are remarkably few tourists and you can spend your time swimming, diving from the mountainside into the pools and watching the abundant wildlife – 90 species of bird alone. It is well worth making the sometimes difficult journey, for it is arguably the most beautiful sight in the whole of Guatemala.

Ingapirca Inca Trail

HOW:
By car and on foot
WHEN TO GO:
Year-round
TIME IT TAKES:
Four days (including getting
to Achupallas, via either the
Valley of Volcanoes or the
Devil's Nose Railway).
HIGHLIGHTS:
Condors wheeling above the
pass at Tres Cruces.
The wilderness beauty of
the yellow, green and grey
grasslands of the paramos,
populated only by fellow-
trekkers and pack mules.
The mighty stones that
make up the 500 year-old
Inca roadway – part of a
continuous system that
extended further than the
Roman Empire's.
Crossing the streams and
swampy valley floor before
Paredones.

The Ingapirca Trail is a 35 km (22 mi) remnant of the
5,000 km (3,125 mi) of well-maintained roads that
united the Inca Empire from Chile to Ecuador. You
reach it by driving southeast of Quito through the
Valley of Volcanoes, a spectacular route that passes
the snow-capped giants of Cotopaxi (5,897 m/19,342
ft), Illinizas (5,263 m/17,263 ft), and Chimborazo,
Ecuador's highest (6,310 m/20,697 ft). Pausing only
for provisions at one of the colourful Indian markets
at Latacunga or Saquisili, you camp at Achupallas, set
3,300 m (10,824 ft) up in the mountains above Alausi.

At first the Inca road follows the Rio Cadrul across
the hills and wild *paramos* (high grasslands) to the
lake at Tres Cruces.
It's clear that in 500
years, nothing very
much can have
changed in the
spectacular landscape.
But above Tres
Cruces, at 4,300 m
(14,104 ft) on the
saddle of the pass and
the trek's highest
point, the panorama is
breathtaking. You can
gaze across the high
peaks in every
direction, and look
down on blue gems of
lakes in the valley
pockets. You camp by
one of them,
Culebrillas, close both
to the Inca ruins of a
tambo (courier rest-

stop) at Paredones, built by the Inca Tupac Yupanqui; and to the quarry where the Incas mined the igneous stone Diorite which they used to build Ingapirca.

Near Ingapirca, the close-set stones show the original Inca roadway to be 7 m (23 ft) wide, a colossal highway through the roof of the world. It's a powerful reminder that the temple to the sun and other buildings at Ingapirca whose walls have been tumbled by wind and grasses, was a mere motel to the culture that built Machu-Picchu. Ingapirca isn't as obviously dramatic as Peru's Inca ruins, but the absence of crowds makes the Inca Trail getting there much more impressive.

YOU SHOULD KNOW:
You must be fully acclimatized to altitude to undertake this moderate to challenging trek, with some previous camping experience.

NEXT: Cotopaxi (front) and Chimborazo (back) volcanoes

The ruins of the Temple of the Sun

Travelling by canoe on the Rio Negro.

Amazon Journey

HOW:
By boat
WHEN TO GO:
In June, the Amazon and Negro reach their flood, which declines until October-November: the igapo rainforest, for example, will have depth variations of 12 m (40 ft). You can travel the Amazon year-round, but each year brings a fresh variation on how best to explore its ecology.
TIME IT TAKES:
5-7 days Iquitos-Manaus (typical 'line boat'); 8-14 days (tour boat, including excursions into the forest). 5-12 days Manaus-Rio Negro-Amazon round trip (various tour boats).

The Amazon is navigable for 4,380 km (2,725 mi) from the Atlantic to the foot of the Peruvian Andes. For 3,600 km (2,240 mi) to Iquitos, it's the dramatic highway for people and freight to cross the continent to Colombia, Ecuador and Peru; and boats of all sizes and degrees of comfort make the trip. But although most travellers can enjoy the experience for itself, they have little opportunity to see anything of the rainforest, its indigenous people, or the unique flora and fauna it hides. The main river, for all its apparent emptiness, has too many settlers on its banks. Instead, from Manaus you can explore the pristine wilderness surrounding the confluence of the Amazon and its biggest tributary the Rio Negro. The Negro's waters are crystal clear, and stained dark with dissolved organic matter; unlike the muddy yellow of the main river, they carry no silt. Where the rivers meet, at Encontra das Aguas, the unified stream flows black and white for more than 32 km (20 mi).

West and north of the confluence the rainforest is almost untouched, and barely inhabited. Over a few days, you can reach deep into all three types – the *igapo*, seasonally flooded with dark water and an orchid-filled, bromeliad-trailing cathedral of fishing birds; *terre firme*, where giant trees with buttresses like rocket fins create the high canopy for howlers and other monkeys; and the *varzea*, flooded with rich silts and with a totally distinct flora that attracts large concentrations of birds, mammals and black caiman. You may be able to visit a deep-forest settlement, and learn something of the medicines as well as nourishment provided by the jungle, or stalk birds on aerial walkways 37 m (120 ft) up in the canopy. These are the things that distinguish adventure from a mainstream Amazon journey.

HIGHLIGHTS:
Lazing in a hammock in the humid languor of midstream Amazon, overflown by blue and gold macaws.
Threading the Anavilhanas Archipelago on the Rio Negro, within constant touching distance of dense unfettered wilderness.
YOU SHOULD KNOW:
Whatever kind of boat you choose, and wherever your destination along the Amazon, watch out for your baggage in every port.

An aerial view of the Rio Negro as it winds through the rainforest.

Patagonia

Few places in the world have captivated the imagination of explorers and travellers like Patagonia. Since Ferdinand Magellan sailed here many have settled, and yet this vast, remote region is still, for the most part, unexplored and largely uninhabited.

Patagonia's beautiful, untamed landscape consists of narrow straits and steep-sided fjords rich in marine life, rugged mountains, harsh, windswept plateaux and glacial valleys. It is home to some of the most beautiful natural attractions in the world, from the granite towers of Torres del Paine and Los Glaciares national parks to the northern and southern ice fields with their enormous glaciers, the flat pampa broken only by bluffs of multi-coloured sedimentary rocks and stunning emerald lakes and rivers.

Considering its size and variety of terrain, Patagonia is surprisingly easy to navigate. One of the most spectacular areas is the Lake District in Argentina which is broken into two regions; the Northern Lakes and the Southern Lakes.

The Northern Lakes, strung along the foot of the Andes, are bordered by both Chile and Argentina. Trekking is the best way to explore the area as this enables you to reach the summit of many spectacular peaks in addition to seeing the wildflower-strewn valleys and everything in between.

Within the Northern Lakes area lie a number of national parks – the Parque Nacional Nahuel Huapi, situated on the Chilean border and the oldest national park in Argentina, the Parque Nacional Los Arrayanes, which surrounds the picturesque port of La Villa, and the Parque Nacional Los Alerces, one of the least spoiled and most beautiful stretches of the Andes, named after its impressive and rare ancient alerce trees.

The Southern Lakes, stretching down to Los

WHAT IS IT:
A vast unsettled region encompassing a variety of terrains of fantastic beauty.
HIGHLIGHTS:
Trek, raft, ski, drink wine, eat gourmet food and experience lovely hospitality and even lovelier scenery.
DON'T MISS:
A visit to the northern Lake District near the border between Chile and Argentina is unforgettable.
WHEN TO GO:
October to April is the most popular time to visit.

Lago Roca, Los Glaciares National Park

Glaciares National Park, also offer spectacular scenery, with the mighty Moreno and Upsala glaciers, and challenging trekking around Mount Fitzroy.

From dense woods to petrified forests, from deserts

to shoreline, Patagonia offers something for everyone, literally from the heights of the Andes, down to what many consider to be the southernmost city in the world, Ushuaia.

Wild horses and Mount Fitzroy

Cape York Peninsula

HOW:
By bike or 4x4
WHEN TO GO:
Dry season (May to October)
TIME IT TAKES:
Three weeks, including rest days. By 4x4, allow one week, including breaks and detours. Make sure you have the right equipment and spares as paying for repairs and breakdowns in remote areas can be very expensive.

The northernmost point of the Australian continent, lonely and remote, Cape York Peninsula has been described as one of the last great wild places on earth. The so-called 'Trip to the Tip' is a challenging one whichever mode of overland transport you choose. If you have the stamina and confidence, one of the best ways to encounter a landscape largely untouched by human hand is by mountain bike. Cairns is the place to organize your own transport or else sign up for an escorted tour. If you travel independently you should bear in mind that accommodation options are limited, so you need to take basic camping equipment as well

as appropriate spares and supplies.

Most of the 1,000 km (625 mi) from Cairns to the Cape is on dirt tracks and unsealed roads. Whilst you have to be on constant alert for potholes and the heavy corrugations that form on many surfaces, you will find your progress is often not much slower than fellow travellers in motor vehicles. And your greater lightness and flexibility will give you the advantage when negotiating the many creek crossings with their swift-flowing streams and steepsided banks.

The route from Cairns takes you up the coast through the Daintree Rainforest and on to Cape Tribulation and Cooktown, before heading inland across Lakefield National Park to join the main road

HIGHLIGHTS:
Camping beneath the paperbark trees on the bank of the Archer River.
The detour to the Iron Range National Park on the east coast of the peninsula, which protects a rainforest eco-system of worldwide importance and where you have your best chance of spotting a cassowary.
Visiting Thursday Island in the Torres Strait by ferry – still Australia but a different world.

Cape Tribulation National Park

running up the spine of the peninsula. The 160 km (100 mi) from the Wenlock River north to the Jardine River, which follows the route of the old Overland Telegraph Line, is a particularly exciting section. After a ferry crossing of the mighty Jardine River it is a relatively straightforward ride, via the small Torres Strait Islander town of Bamaga to Cape York itself, where a sign confirms you are at the tip of mainland Australia.

ABOVE: A boardwalk in the Daintree Rainforest

RIGHT: Dancer at the Laura Aboriginal Dance Festival

Punakaiki Horseback Ride

HOW:
On horseback
WHEN TO GO:
Any time of year (just be
sure to pick a fine day!)
TIME IT TAKES:
The standard ride takes
around 2.5 hours.
HIGHLIGHTS:
Getting to (and going on
from) Punakaiki along one of
the most spectacular
coastal highways in New
Zealand, between the sea
and Southern Alps.
The fascinating surge pool
at Dolomite Point – known
as the Devil's Cauldron, it
can have a mesmeric effect.
With luck – spotting a pod of
Hector's Dolphins disporting
themselves just off Pancake
Rocks.
YOU SHOULD KNOW:
The three blowholes at
Dolomite Point put on their
best show when there is a
strong southwesterly swell
at high tide.

Between the towns of Westport and Greymouth on the South Island's west coast is Paparoa National Park, alongside State Highway 6. This is a land of extraordinary coastline, lush coastal forests, canyons and limestone cliffs, caves and underground streams.

One of the most notable features is the famous Pancake Rocks and accompanying blowholes of Dolomite Point near the small settlement of Punakaiki. The most invigorating way of appreciating these amazing natural phenomena is to see them from horseback after a ride through the heart of the scenic Punakaiki Valley. The local stables offers a variety of custom rides to suit individual requirements, but also run a popular standard short excursion that gives a wonderful flavour of Paparoa National Park's unique attractions. The horses are steady and it is possible to enjoy the trek without having previous riding experience (elementary tuition is given).

It begins with an atmospheric ride into the Punakaiki Valley, fording the river and passing through native bush to view huge limestone bluffs topped with temperate rainforest. Abundant birdlife is a feature of the Park, and birds seem less cautious when the watchers are on horseback. Species to look out for are whitebreasted native kereru (pigeons), the bright pukeko, inquisitive weka, paradise duck, spur-winged plover and harrier hawk.

There will be a short rest stop at a bush hut on the river flats, before returning to the coast and riding along Punakaiki Beach, with horses strolling through the seething white water at the water's edge. The climax of the ride is simply sitting and marvelling as the powerful sea crashes into the Pancake Rocks and erupts upwards through the blowholes. This expanse of water-sculpted grey rock resembles endless stacks of pancakes forming a fabulous tableau – can't be eaten, but never forgotten!

The Pancake Rocks at Dolomite Point

REST & RELAXATION
ESCAPES

Ven

WHEN TO GO:
May to September
HOW TO GET THERE:
Ferry from Landskrona on
the Swedish mainland
several times a day; and from
Helsingborg and Copenhagen
in the summer only
HIGHLIGHTS:
Brahe Observatory and
Museum – dedicated to
Tycho Brahe.
The distillery and whisky bar
at Backafallsbyn – the largest
collection of single malts in
Sweden.

*PREVIOUS: Monastery
at Vis Harbour, Croatia*

The Pearl of Oresund is a tiny dot in the strait between
Sweden and Denmark, 8 km (5 mi) off the Danish coast
and just 4.3 km (under 3 mi) from Sweden. It is only
7.5 sq km (3 sq mi), a shelf that slopes downward south
to north from its highest point at 45 m (150 ft) to just 5
m (16 ft) above sea level. The island is incredibly fertile
farmland with rich clay topsoil on layers of shifting sand
and clay.

Ven belonged to Denmark until 1660 when it fell into
Swedish hands. During the 16th century, Tycho Brahe, a
famous Danish astronomer, persuaded the king of
Denmark to give him the island so that he could study
the stars from here. He built a Baroque castle, now in
ruins, and for the next 20 years took measurements of
the night skies, incredibly precisely considering his
primitive equipment.

When you go ashore from the ferry at Bäckviken, the grassy slopes of the celebrated Backafall cliffs rise straight out of the sea 40 m (130 ft) high, giving amazing views over the Oresund to the Danish and Swedish coasts. Kyrkbacken, the oldest and largest harbour with a yachting marina, is a pretty village with a fish smokery. There are sand beaches near both harbours.

Ven is a lovely island for camping and cycling holidays. Paths cut through the fields and copses so that you can wander freely everywhere. Coastal walks take you along some hair-raising cliff tops where you will see dramatic landslips and down to curious rocky shores full of marine life. Artists and craftsmen have been attracted here by the inspiring tranquillity and you can visit their studios and workshops. The bucolic surroundings, sea views, lively harbours, and sense of history make it an ideal place for anyone seeking a relaxing island break.

St Ibbs Church – dating back to the 13th century in a lovely spot above Kyrkbacken village.

Nämndemansgården farm – the oldest farmstead on the island; now a heritage museum.

Eating the island's pasta – a Ven speciality made from locally produced durum wheat.

YOU SHOULD KNOW:
The cliffs are heavily eroded in some places and you should be careful when walking along them.

Fertile farmland makes great scenery for cyclists.

Åland Islands

WHEN TO GO:
May to August for sunshine, December to February for winter sports

HOW TO GET THERE:
By boat from Grisslehamn or Kapellskär in Sweden, or from Turku in Finland. Fly from Helsinki, Turku or Stockholm.

HIGHLIGHTS:
Exploring the islands and islets in a rowing boat, and discovering the beautiful deserted beaches.
The *Pommern* – an historic sailing ship built in Glasgow at the beginning of the last century, now on display at Mariehamn.
The Bomarsund – the great Russian fortress destroyed by French and British marines during the Crimean War.

YOU SHOULD KNOW:
Despite being under Finnish sovereignty, the language spoken here is Swedish.

In the clear blue waters of the Baltic at the mouth of the Gulf of Bothnia, Åland is an archipelago consisting of around 80 inhabited emerald islands plus 6000 smaller islets and rocks. Officially belonging to Finland, the islands were awarded a wide degree of autonomy by the League of Nations in 1921 to settle a long-running dispute between Sweden and Finland. Åland has its own government, its own flag, its own stamps and its own vehicle licence plates.

Most visitors come here for the slow pace of life and the tranquil beauty of the archipelago. The best way to explore the islands is by rowing boat. You'll soon find a beach all to yourself – perhaps even a whole island.

Fasta Åland is the largest island in the archipelago, with an area of around 1,000 sq km (600 sq mi). Here can be found Mariehamn, the only town in the archipelago, where just under half of the population of the islands live. Founded in 1861, Mariehamn is the centre of the shipping and tourist industries and home to the Landskapsregering – the local seat of government.

In the summer months, from May to August, the Åland Islands receive more sunshine than any of their Nordic neighbours, making them a popular holiday destination. In winter, visitors come for the long-distance skating or to experience ice-boating through the ice-sheets that form around the smaller islands and skerries.

At any time of the year there are various cultural highlights to entertain visitors, including the Kastelholm. This medieval castle, mostly a ruin today, was home to many Swedish kings who ruled the combined kingdom of Sweden and Finland. The great fortress of Bomarsund was built by the Russians in 1832, but later destroyed by British and French warships in 1854 as part of the campaign in the Baltic during the Crimean War. On the other side of the channel there is a small museum with pictures and objects from the Bomarsund.

Mariehamn's Maritime Quarter is also worth a visit, where you can see traditional boat-building, a smithy and other local handicrafts. The marina accommodates small ships and traditional wooden boats. The Maritime Museum contains exhibitions of historic and contemporary boat-building.

NEXT: One of many deserted bays to discover by rowing boat.

An idyllic dwelling on the Åland Islands, with the boathouse in the background.

Hiddensee

WHEN TO GO:
The high season runs from
May to September but the
island caters for tourists
throughout the year.
HOW TO GET THERE:
Ferry from Stralsund on the
mainland (2 hours) or
Schaprode on the island of
Rügen (45 mins) several
times a day.
HIGHLIGHTS:
Inselkirche – the island
church and graveyard in
Kloster.
Gellen sandbank – shifting
sand dunes in the south of
island for bird watching,
part of the
Boddenlandschaft National
Park, which has Europe's
biggest crane roost –
around 30,000 fly in every
August.
YOU SHOULD KNOW:
You must book months in
advance to get a hotel room
between June and August;
camping is not permitted
anywhere on the island.
There is a daily 'spa tax',
collected by your landlord
or, for day-trippers, by the
ferry company.

This sliver of land, clinging to the west coast of the island of Rügen on Germany's Baltic coast, has preserved all the charm that attracted so many famous early 20th century artists, writers and intellectuals to its shores, including Einstein, Freud, Brecht and Thomas Mann.

Hiddensee is less than 17 km (11 mi) long and just 250 m (820 ft) wide at its narrowest point. The landscape is exceptionally beautiful with incredibly varied scenery – precipitous rocks contrasting with the wide sandy beaches, meadows and saltmarshes, huge dunes, sandflats and undulating heathland. Large parts of the island are only just above sea level while the highest point is 72 m (236 ft). The broad white sands along the western and north coasts, stretching for some 16 km (10 mi), are some of the finest anywhere in the world; only the chilly Baltic wind reminds you

*The beaches are some of
the finest anywhere.*

that you are not in the Caribbean. No cars are allowed here. Transport is provided by horse-drawn carriages or bicycles. The main town, Vitte, is a small port on the east coast just to the north of the Dünenheide, a beautiful area of heathland which in August is a blazing purple carpet of heather. The only other sizeable settlement is the unspoilt little village of Kloster on the north coast, which grew from a Cistercian monastery established in 1296.

Hiddensee has a faintly bohemian atmosphere – a retreat for individualists seeking peace from the madding crowd. It is still known as an artists' haunt and you will stumble across small galleries and roadside exhibitions wherever you go. Although there are loads of day-trippers in the summer months, it is not hard to escape by walking just that little bit further to find yourself surrounded by a seemingly unending expanse of sea and sky with a feeling of unbounded space. Absolute bliss!

NEXT: The lighthouse at Schluckwieck

HOW TO GET THERE:
By ferry from Quiberon (year round) or from Vannes (summer only).

WHEN TO GO:
Spring and autumn are less busy.

HIGHLIGHTS:
Musée Historique – housed in the citadel at Le Palais, it records the island's often turbulent history.
Grotte de l'Apothicairerie – a spectacular coastal cavern.
Storm-watching at Pointe des Poulains – the island's most northerly point.
The cave system at Aiguilles de Port-Coton.

YOU SHOULD KNOW:
The British navy captured Belle Ile in 1761, but two years later swapped it for the Mediterranean island of Menorca.

Belle Ile

As the name suggests this is a truly beautiful island. A combination of a rugged coastline, attractive fishing villages and white sandy beaches, has made it a magnet for summer tourists. In July and August the population can increase ten-fold, all crammed into 84 sq km (36 sq mi). However, even in peak times, it is possible to lose oneself on this island of contrasts. The

deeply eroded south-west is a true Côte Sauvage (wild coast), while the sheltered eastern side can feel positively Mediterranean in spite of its Atlantic location.

Belle Ile's history is closely linked both to the English, who occupied the island for two years, from 1761 to 1763, during the Seven Years War, and the Acadians, who took refuge on the island when the English got the upper hand in France's Canadian colonies.

The Plage des Grands Sables

A sailing boat anchored in the cove at Port Goulphar.

Now the island is known for the more traditional pleasures of any vacation on the Brittany coast: swimming, boating, fishing, cycling and hiking. It also houses a collection of attractive lighthouses, most notably Le Grand Phare on the west coast, and La Citadelle Vauban, one of a series of substantial 17th century military fortresses built for Louis XIV by Marshal Vauban and now turned into an historical museum.

The island has long attracted the attentions of the world's best artists. Inspired by its natural splendour, Monet, Van Gogh and Henri Matisse amongst others produced some of their finest work here. The island is also said to have inspired the Op Art movement of the 1950s when the Hungarian-born artist Victor Vasarely visited and was inspired by the shapes of the pebbles on the beach at Sauzon.

Belle Ile boasts one of the best hiking routes in Europe. The spectacular 95 km (60 mi) coastal path takes about a week to complete and there are ample *gîtes d'étape* (walkers' hostels) and campsites en route.

Caldey Island

Caldey Island, which lies 5 km (3 mi) off the south coast of Pembrokeshire, is one of Britain's holy islands. Only 2.4 km (1.5 mi) long and 1.6 km (1 mi) wide, it has been inhabited since the Stone Age, and since Celtic times it has been inhabited by monks.

A Celtic monastery was founded here by Pyro, in the 6th century, and the Old Priory is believed to have been built on that original site. During the 10th century, Viking raids are thought to have put an end to the monastic settlement, but 200 years later Benedictines from St Dogmaels in Pembrokeshire built a Priory here, where they remained until the Dissolution of the Monasteries in 1536. In 1906 Anglican Benedictines bought Caldey and the Abbott, Aelred Carlyle,

WHEN TO GO:
From Easter to the end of October.
HOW TO GET THERE:
Boats run from Tenby Harbour at high tide, and Castle Beach landing stage at low tide. Boats don't sail on Sundays.

A detail of a stained glass window in St David's Church

HIGHLIGHTS:
St Illtyd's Church and the
Old Priory.
Attending Mass in the
Abbott's Chapel and touring
the monastery (men only).
The Caldey Stone, inscribed
in both Celtic and Latin.
St. Margarets, Caldey's
sister island (joined at low
tide) – a seal and bird
sanctuary.
Visiting the Post Office and
Museum, and having a
postcard franked with
Caldey's unique imprint.
YOU SHOULD KNOW:
The Caldey Island
monastery provides
spiritual retreats throughout
the year for both men and
women (though only men
are permitted to enter the
main building), and it is
possible to stay on the
island.

commissioned the beautiful Italianate Abbey from architect John Coates-Carter. Unable to make ends meet, the Benedictines sold the Abbey to Cistercian monks, Trappists, in 1926, where they remain peacefully ensconced in what is now a Grade II* listed building.

Although Caldey is best known for its monastery, it has a pretty village, too. Here one can buy a number of things made on the island, which provide an income for the monks. Farming produces milk, butter and cream and the monks produce yoghurt, ice-cream, shortbread and

A view of monastic Caldey Island

chocolate, which are on sale in the village. Their most famous product, however, is a range of perfumes and skin creams, made from Caldey's flowers, herbs and gorse.

This is a wonderful place to visit, with a uniquely serene and tranquil atmosphere. Quiet and unpolluted, with no traffic to disturb the peace, Caldey can be explored on foot. From the gorgeous Priory Beach to the lighthouse at the summit of the island, magnificent views over the south coast of Pembrokeshire can be enjoyed.

Islay

WHEN TO GO:
Any time
HOW TO GET THERE:
By ferry from Kennacraig in West Loch Tarbert, or by air from Glasgow.
HIGHLIGHTS:
The National Nature Reserve at Duich Moss.
The Islay Festival of Malt and Music, held each late May/early June.
The Museum of Islay Life at Port Charlotte.
The ancient burial grounds at Nerabus, containing wonderful medieval gravestones.
The island of Jura, a five-minute ferry journey from Islay, this wild, mountainous island is fantastic for hill walking.
YOU SHOULD KNOW:
Portnahaven, a charming fishing village 11 km (7 mi) south of Port Charlotte, is home to the world's first commercial wave-powered generating station. Known as 'Limpet', it powers 200 homes on the island.

The green, hilly island of Islay was, in medieval times, the capital of the Western Isles. Today, Islay is synonymous with its unique, peaty, single malt whisky, and the island is home to eight separate distilleries. Between them they produce some four million gallons of whisky per year, much of which is exported. Most visitors come for the whiskey trail, leaving the rest of the island relatively unknown. The remainder come for the birds because, between October and April, Islay is a destination on the migration route of thousands of white fronted and barnacle geese, flying south from Greenland for the winter.

Islay is always windy, but fairly mild, and the land is fertile. There is moorland, woods, machair, sea lochs and a rugged coastline with great expanses of beach. Inhabited since Neolithic times, there is much here to interest archaeologists, for example the Kildalton High Cross, often considered to be the finest in Scotland, which was carved from bluestone in 800 AD. Close to the cross are some remarkably carved, 15th century gravestones, and further on, at Trudernish Point are standing stones.

The Paps of Jura mountains

The island's main centre of population and ferry port is Port Ellen, which was planned and laid out in the 1820s. An attractive town, its own distillery dominates the skyline, though it is no longer operational. Nearby, however, are three very well-known distilleries: Laphroig, Lagavulin and Ardbeg, beautifully situated and fun to visit.

At Laphroig you not only see the malting but also the peat kilns. Bowmore, on the east side of Loch Indaal, is Islay's current 'capital', and home to its eponymous oldest distillery, started in 1779. Port Charlotte, on the west of Loch Indaal is probably Islay's prettiest village, and makes a good base for a few days.

NEXT: An Islay deer stands against the rugged landscape.

Vis

WHEN TO GO:
Mid-June to mid-September
HOW TO GET THERE:
Fly to Split, then ferry or
hydrofoil from Split or the
islands of Korcula or Hvar.
HIGHLIGHTS:
The Archaeological Museum.
Zelena Spilja – an emerald
cave near Rukavak Bay.
The 16th century St Cyprian
Church.
Uvala Stoncica and Uvala
Stiniva – delightful small
coves.
YOU SHOULD KNOW:
For centuries Vis has been
famous for its viticulture.

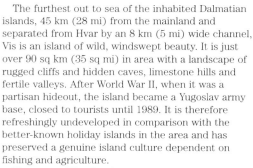

RIGHT: Vis seen from the Monastery.

A view out to sea from Komiza

The furthest out to sea of the inhabited Dalmatian islands, 45 km (28 mi) from the mainland and separated from Hvar by an 8 km (5 mi) wide channel, Vis is an island of wild, windswept beauty. It is just over 90 sq km (35 sq mi) in area with a landscape of rugged cliffs and hidden caves, limestone hills and fertile valleys. After World War II, when it was a partisan hideout, the island became a Yugoslav army base, closed to tourists until 1989. It is therefore refreshingly undeveloped in comparison with the better-known holiday islands in the area and has preserved a genuine island culture dependent on fishing and agriculture.

The town of Vis (Issa) on the north-eastern coast of the island is the oldest urban settlement on the Adriatic. Inhabited since 3000 BC, the island was colonized by Greeks from Sicily who established a *polis* (democratic city-state). It is estimated that the city had 12,000 to 14,000 inhabitants and was therefore a place of enormous significance. You can still see Greek and Roman ruins here as well as some lovely 16th and 17th century churches and villas. On the west coast, the 17th century fishing village of Komiza, with its Renaissance citadel and monastery is in a huge sandy-bottomed bay. This picturesque village is a motley jumble of houses huddled round a harbour at the foot of Hum, the highest hill on the island at 587 m (1,925 ft). As well as its beautiful wild mountain scenery and unspoiled cultural heritage there are some beautiful beaches, the best known being Zaglav, 10 km (6 mi) south of Vis Town. There is also superb paragliding here and some great diving sites, with six sunken wrecks dating from ancient times to World War II.

Blue Voyage

Cevat Sakir Kabaagac, a Bodrum writer, recounted his travels by boat around the Carian and Lycian coasts and now the title of his book *Blue Voyage*, describes cruises in these Turkish waters. With rocky coastlines backed by dramatic forested mountains and waters of heavenly peacock hues, this is an idyllic region for a leisurely sea-voyage.

Gulets are graceful traditional Turkish motoryachts,

still constructed locally of the red pine that covers the hillsides. Most are now built for the tourist business and they're comfortable and well equipped. They may be chartered by groups, or a cruise can be an alternative 'package' holiday.

A typical Blue Voyage will sail from Bodrum to Marmaris by way of pretty Gökova, mooring here or at one of the neighbouring fishing villages or coves, and along the north of the narrow Datça Peninsula, doubling back to Datça, with its busy harbour and

Two gulets moored in Tuzla Bay

Castle of St Peter at Bodrum

waterfront. Fjordlike Keci Buku Bay provides anchorage on the journey east to Marmaris, at the traditional fishing village of Selimye, or Bozburun, renowned for its boat building. Just short of huge, hectic Marmaris lie the more tranquil bays of Turunc and Kumlubük. The gulet will be at sea for several hours each day – possibly under sail – anchoring for swimming, visiting fishing villages or, for those with an interest in history, archaeological sites. The captain will establish his passengers' preferences. Scattered around the Gulf of Gökova are the remains of several ancient towns; the ancient city of Cnidos lies at the tip of the Datça Peninsula, and on a promontory south of Bozburun are the ruins of Loryma, with its sheltered harbour.

Lake Balkhash

The vast scimitar-shaped Lake Balkhash is the second largest lake in area in Central Asia. Strangely, it is salty in the east and fresh water in the west, and is deeper in the eastern arm although its maximum depth is only about 27 m (90 ft) and its surface is usually frozen solid from November to March. Its surface area is currently 17,580 sq km (7000 sq mi) and it is at 14 m (47 ft) below sea level. It is an endorheic lake; that is, it loses water by evaporation as it has no outflow. The two halves of the lake are separated by a sandbar and the main inflow is from the River Ili in the west. Lake Balkhash is a vital stopping point for birds during the migrating seasons and the area is becoming increasingly popular with western birdwatchers. The reedbeds of the Ili delta are thought to be among the best places to see various rarities, including Dalmatian and white pelicans, several species of terns, spoonbills, night herons, feruginous duck and white-tailed eagle, although there are also other spots on the lake from where many of these can be seen. Away from the populated coastal towns and cities like Balkhash, this beautiful, wild landscape is a peaceful place to visit.

WHAT IS IT:
An unusual lake in eastern Kazakhstan
HOW TO GET THERE:
By road from Almaty
WHEN TO GO:
Spring or autumn
NEAREST TOWN:
Balkhash

Lake Balkhash stretches across the horizon.

Bazaruto Archipelago

WHEN TO GO:
Year round, but avoid the cyclone season in February. Little rainfall between April and November.

HOW TO GET THERE:
Flights into Viklankulo (sometimes via Maputo) with connections on to the archipelago.

HIGHLIGHTS:
Marlin fishing from mid-September to the end of December. Sailfish fishing from April to August, and fishing for smaller game fish such as king mackerel, bonito and travelli all year round.
Birdwatching – sunbirds, bee-eaters, paradise flycatchers and crab plovers.
Shell-seeking for the famous 'Pansy Shells' at North Point, Pansy Island and various sand dunes.
Dining out on freshly caught fish, cooked in the Portuguese style.

YOU SHOULD KNOW:
The locals use the husks from the harvested cashews to make very intoxicating liquor.

Halfway up the Mozambique coast lies a chain of five islands making up the Bazaruto Archipelago. Formed from sand deposited by the Limpopo River, fine beaches and coral reefs come naturally; and having long been a national park, so does the wildlife. Bazaruto, Benguerra and Magaruque are the largest islands, with Santa Carolina and finally Bangué coming in on the small side.

Thanks to their protected status and relative isolation from the ravages of war, nature has been free to flourish here; and bizarre yet endearing dugongs, or sea cows, spend their days grazing among seagrass meadows offshore. Bazurato Island itself is 37 km (23 mi) long, and here gaudy pink flamingoes strut the tidal flats, while large Nile crocodiles lurk in the inland freshwater lakes. The west is cloaked in grassland and thicket while the east coast is built entirely of impressive sand dunes. Benguerra is about 11 km (7 mi) long and its blend of forest, savannah and wetlands provides rich pickings for local wildlife. Cashew nuts are native to the island and grow mainly on the seaward side.

Wild orange trees and sisal trees abound, as do mlala palms – the leaves of which are used in the weaving of mats, baskets and hats. Nature lovers, sun worshippers and water sports enthusiasts alike are drawn here. It may be said of other places, but this is as close as it gets to a true tropical paradise. With clear turquoise waters and endless palm-dotted beaches, this is the place to escape from the pressures of everyday life – to snorkel and surf, and run coral pink sand through your fingers. There are no roads, no shops and no tourist attractions to divert you from the serious business of relaxing.

NEXT: Local fisherman set sail to catch dinner.

Pink beaches and turquoise water as far as the eye can see!

Prince Edward Island

WHEN TO GO:
Most attractions open from Victoria Day (in May) to Thanksgiving (early October). The island is less crowded and more spectacular in the autumn months.

HOW TO GET THERE:
Fly to Charlottetown, ferry to Wood Islands from Nova Scotia or across the Confederation Bridge.

HIGHLIGHTS:
Green Gables House near Cavendish – the setting for the famous book.
Hiking up and down the craggy coastline in Brundenell River Provincial Park.

Pink and purple wild lupins grow freely on the island.

The crescent-shaped Prince Edward Island (PEI) is the smallest Canadian province. Its area of 5,520 sq km (2,184 sq mi) makes it even smaller than some of Canada's National Parks, but also allows it to be explored in less than a week. The island lies in the Gulf of St Lawrence, separated from the northern coasts of the Maritime Provinces of New Brunswick and Nova Scotia by the narrow Northumberland Strait.

The Mi'kmaq people, original inhabitants of PEI called the island Abegweit, meaning 'Land Cradled on the Waves'; they believed that it was formed by the Great Spirit throwing some red clay into the sea. In 1534 the French explorer Jacques Cartier laid claim to the island but by the end of the eighteenth century the British were in control. They expelled the Acadians and named the island after Queen Victoria's father, Prince Edward. The islanders maintained a sense of independence until the Charlottetown Conference of 1864 when Canada was born, earning PEI the epithet 'Cradle of the Confederation'.

Ploughed potato fields stretch towards the sea.

PEI is a well-known haven of peace and tranquillity for those seeking a place to get away from it all. The islanders are warm and welcoming. The nature here seems to possess a serene quality, with expansive undulating hills where rich green and ruddy farmland offer up a pleasant patchwork of colour. Dotting this gentle landscape are little hamlets, where the tempo has remained unchanged by the rigours of modern life. Like their Mi'kmaq predecessors, many of today's islanders draw their livelihood from agriculture and fishing.

This is a land of plenty with bountiful harvests from land and sea, famous for its oysters, mussels and, above all, lobsters. It boasts beautiful lighthouses, tree-lined streets and 19th century terraces, as well as coves, parks, rocky headlands and long sandy beaches.

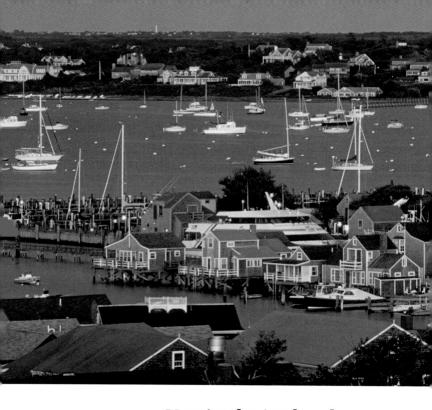

Nantucket harbour in the foreground with the multi-million dollar summer houses across the water in Monomoy.

Nantucket Island

The English explorer Bartholomew Gosnold put Nantucket Island on the map in 1602 when he passed by on the Dartmouth bark *Concord*.

This Massachusetts island off Cape Cod is nicknamed the 'Grey Lady' (it often rains). Nantucket was settled by the English from the 1660s, going on to

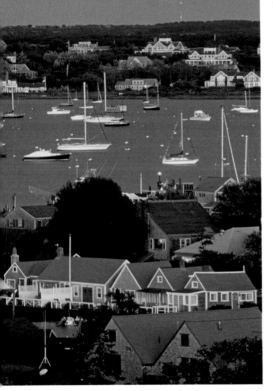

WHEN TO GO:
Most attractions are open in summer season only (June-October), though the island is beautiful all year round.
HOW TO GET THERE:
A choice of three ferry services from the mainland or light aircraft to the busy Nantucket Memorial Airport.
HIGHLIGHTS:
Historic Nantucket Town, for a real sense of a long-vanished New England way of life.
The Whaling Museum, run by the Nantucket Historical Association.
Seal Encounter Cruises from Nantucket harbour to remote Tuckernuck and Muskeget Islands.
The Nantucket Life Saving Museum, providing a fascinating tribute to the early islanders who saved countless lives in the treacherous waters around Nantucket.
Beaches – Nantucket has lots of them, all sandy, all pristine.
YOU SHOULD KNOW:
A key acronym on Nantucket and neighbouring Martha's Vineyard is BYOB. If you want to eat out (or drink in), bring your own bottle – no booze for sale here!

become the world's leading whaling port. The industry faded throughout the 19th century and the community declined, a process hastened by a destructive whale oil fire in 1846 that destroyed much of the town. This ultimately proved to be the island's salvation, as a hundred years of isolation and stagnation meant that very little changed on Nantucket after the Civil War era. When enterprising developers moved in after World War II, they had the

ante-bellum buildings was an asset to be restored rather than something to be swept away and replaced with modern development. Strict controls have maintained this policy ever since, with the result that there's little tackiness evident on this up-market summer resort island. The Nantucket Historical Association maintains six wonderful properties that represent the island's preserved heritage, including the oldest house (built 1686), the Old Gaol and Quaker Meeting house built in 1838 to serve the island's most prominent religion.

A climbing rose blooms on the side of a house in Siasconset.

The island has an area of just 124 sq km (48 sq mi). The main settlement is also called Nantucket which lies beside the harbour at the western end. Other notable localities are Madaket, Miacomet, Polpis, Siasconset, Surfside and Wauwinet.

Much of the northeastern seaboard aims to offer the sort of idealized, laid-back beach holidays amidst traditional New England architecture that have almost become part of the American Dream (summer section). Inexorable commercial pressures have made such simple pleasures harder to find, but Nantucket delivers in spades.

LEFT: Brant Point Light, the second oldest lighthouse in the United States

Tangier Island

WHEN TO GO:
Access is easiest in the summer months and winters can be very hard.
HOW TO GET THERE:
There is a landing strip for air taxis, ferry services from the mainland (Crisfield, Maryland and two Virginia ports, Onancock and Reedville), plus island boat cruises.

This isolated island in Chesapeake Bay is part of Accomack County, Virginia, and is separated from the Bay's eastern shore by Pocomoke Sound. It is tiny, with an area of just 0.6 sq km (0.2 sq mi). Its first known explorer was Captain John Smith of Pocahontas fame, and the island passed through various hands in the 1600s.

In fact, Tangier Island is a series of long islets divided by marsh and small tidal streams. These are all connected by narrow wooden bridges that do not permit the passage of motor vehicles, so the main modes of transport are golf cart, boat, moped, bike and foot. There are three significant ridges – Main Ridge, Canton and West Ridge. The northern part of Main Ridge is quaintly named Me at Soup. Other island districts are Black Dye, Sheep's Head and Hog Ridge.

Watermen collecting oysters in the bay.

The two words that best describe the island are 'old' and 'fashioned'. The tough and independent inhabitants speak a unique dialect thought to be unchanged since its first occupation by English colonists. There is one payphone, no ATM and the few tourist facilities have only recently started accepting credit cards. That said, the island is modernizing fast with the arrival of cable TV – a process not to everyone's liking. Tourism supplements the island's main economic activity – soft shell crabbing and oyster fishing. Men tend to focus on the latter, leaving the women to deal with tourists.

There are bed-and-breakfast establishments offering overnight stays, but most visitors come as part of an organized tour, or take a day-trip to the island by regular ferry. Upon arrival, they find a few gift shops, eateries (crab cakes a speciality), one general store...and an island with unique character.

HIGHLIGHTS:
Spanky's 1950s-style ice-cream parlour on Main Ridge.
Birds – thousands of pelicans, blue herons, egrets, rails, osprey, ducks and geese attracted by rich marshland.

YOU SHOULD KNOW:
Tangier islanders only abandoned the practice of burying their dead beneath the family lawn in the early 20th century, when most of the small yards became fully occupied.

117

Cat Island

WHEN TO GO:
Any time of year
HOW TO GET THERE:
Fly from Fort Lauderdale or
the other islands in the
Bahamas, or mailboat from
Nassau on New Providence
Island.
HIGHLIGHTS:
The Hermitage – a
monastery on Mount
Alvernia, the highest point in
the Bahamas
The glorious stretches of
pink and white sandy
beaches
Snorkelling and diving in the
clear waters
The crumbling mansions on
the old cotton plantations
as a reminder of the past.
YOU SHOULD KNOW:
This is said to be Columbus'
original landing site in the
New World.

Located between Eleuthera and Long Island, Cat Island is the sixth largest island in the Bahamas at 77 km (48 mi) long and 2-7 km (1-4 mi) wide. Unlike many other islands in the chain, Cat Island is definitely low key when it comes to tourism, despite the 97 km (60 mi) of deserted pink and white sand beaches which surround it. This is one of the most beautiful and lush of the islands. From its high cliffs there's a stunning view of the densely forested foothills of Mount Alvernia. This is the highest point on Cat Island, and the highest point in the Bahamas, albeit at just 63 m (206 ft) above sea level. At the summit of Mount Alvernia is a monastery called The Hermitage, hewn from the limestone cliffs by Father Jerome, a penitent hermit, as a place for meditation.

There are two theories on the naming of the island. Some believe it was named after Arthur Catt, the famous British sea captain, others that it got its name from the hordes of feral cats the English discovered when they arrived in the 17th century. The cats were said to be descendants of those left behind by early Spanish colonists as they passed through on their way to find the gold of South America.

The first permanent settlement on Cat Island was made in 1783 by cotton planters who brought wealth to the island. Now the crumbling remains of their mansions, as well as the associated slave villages, stand among the wild tropical flowers and grasses. One such plantation is at Port Howe, a pretty village said to have been built by the intrepid Colonel Andrew Deveaux who recaptured Nassau from the Spanish in 1783. Many descendants of the original early settlers remain on the island today, including actor Sidney Poitier who spent his youth in Arthur's Town and later returned to settle here. The island may have gained wealth from cotton plantations in the

The Hermitage on
Mount Alvernia

past, but slash and burn farming is now the main way of life for Cat Islanders. Many grow cascarilla bark as a cash crop, which is gathered and shipped to Italy where it becomes a main ingredient in medicines, perfumes and Campari.

Much of the folklore of the Bahamas originates on

Cat Island. Traditionally, when the last remaining person of a generation dies, his or her house is left empty for the spirit to live in. The person's relatives gather stones from the site to make a new house. In the north of the island, some people still place spindles on top of their houses to ward off harm.

A pristine beach on Fernandez Bay

Saona

Off the southeast tip of the Dominican Republic, where the Atlantic and the Caribbean go head to head, lies the incarnation of the tropical island idyll. Its curves of white sand fringed by swaying palm trees, green against the azure sea, combine in a single image celebrated by millions of Europeans as the setting for the Bounty (chocolate) Bar TV commercial. Saona is the notion of paradise made manifest – and it looks even better than on film.

There are just two tiny settlements on the 25 km (15 mi) by 5 km (3 mi) island. Punta Gorda and the picturesque fishing village of Mano Juan are sleepy relics of the trading stations established after 1493 by Colombus, who bullied the Taino chieftain Cotubanamá into an unequal partnership. Cotubanamá's descendants now appear to be exacting an exquisite revenge. After centuries of subsistence fishing, in just ten years they have become unofficial beachmasters to the fleet of speedboats and catamarans that each day bring over hundreds of day-trippers from every major resort on the mainland, to bear witness to the existence in fact of a television dream. But Saona is part of a National Park and Marine Reserve with no amenities except in the tiny, restricted areas allotted to each resort group – where the islanders ply the by now rum-happy tourists with trinkets, curios, 'personalized' photos or video clips and 'massages' to the thumping beats of a beach boom-box.

You can walk away along equally fabulous but empty beaches, to lagoons full of flamingoes and mangroves stirred by pelicans, redfooted boobies, and Hispaniolan lizard-cuckoos and parrots. You can snorkel or dive among giant sponges and teeming fish on the reefs where manatees float in languor and dolphins somersault. The serenity of wonderland is still there – if you want to find it.

WHEN TO GO:
November to June
HOW TO GET THERE:
By catamaran or speedboat from the beach at Bayahibe or Dominicus on the mainland. Most of the boats are pre-booked to resort groups, but there are some independent excursion sellers.
HIGHLIGHTS:
Laguna de los Flamencos near the mangroves in the southwest.
The amazing Arawak and Taino rock art in the Cueva Cotubanamá – the cave in the island's west where the Chief hid before his capture by the Spanish.
'La Piscina Natural' – underwater sandbars hundreds of metres out to sea, where you jump into waist-deep water to drink, party, and frighten the lovely fish. Or just swim.
The photo you take home showing you at the Bounty Bar beach, yes, really!
YOU SHOULD KNOW:
On the big catamarans, someone will come round putting a little hat on your head. They are not being kind – unless you reject it immediately, you will be charged at least US$4 for it on leaving the boat.

Fishermen's cottages line a perfect beach. 123

The Marquesa Islands

HOW TO GET THERE:
Either fly from Papeete or
Rangiroa to Nuku Hiva, the
largest island or take one of
the cruise ships or
freighters that sail monthly
from Papeete, calling at all
six of the inhabited
Marquesas.

WHAT IS THERE TO DO:
Join the dedicated surfers
who come for the waves.

LITERARY CONNECTIONS:
Hermann Melville's *Typee* is
a classic narrative of
nineteenth-century
Marquesan life and Thor
Heyerdahl's *Fatu Hiva* is an
account of his attempt to
'get back to nature'.

The 7,500 inhabitants of the Marquesa Islands could reasonably lay claim to living in the remotest place in the world. Farther from a continental landfall than any other group of islands on Earth, the Marquesas poke out of the open Pacific just south of the equator and about 1,400 km (870 mi) north-east of Tahiti. Unlike many of the islands in the South Pacific, the Marquesas are, because of their remoteness, almost entirely unspoiled. They are wild and rugged islands with steep cliffs and valleys leading up to high central ridges.

Brooding volcanic pinnacles pierce the landscape, while the lush vegetation is overflowing with bougainvillea, orchids, spider lilies, ginger and jasmine, as well as all manner of fruit from grapefruit and banana to mango and papaya.

Of the twelve Marquesa islands, known in the local Polynesian language as 'Land of the Men', only six are

A typical Nuku Hiva landscape

RIGHT: The church at Fatu Hiva

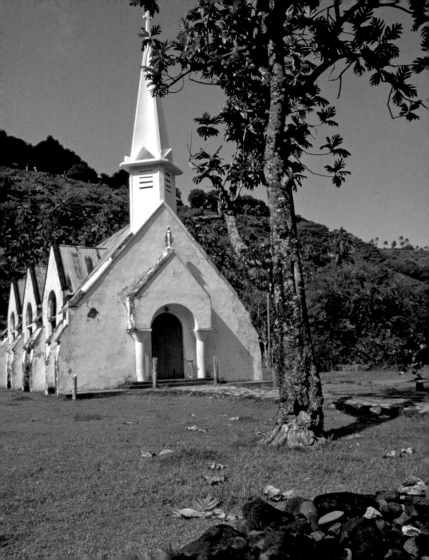

Sailboats anchored in the Bay of Virgins, at Fatu Hiva

inhabited, with most of the population living in the narrow fertile valleys, leaving the interiors to the hundreds of wild horses, cattle and goats. The birdlife is extraordinarily rich and varied and the waters around the islands are teeming with fish and lobsters. The size and quality of the ocean waves as they reach many of the beaches of the Marquesas make the islands a hot spot for surfers. The town of Atuona on Hiva Oa, the second largest island, is famous as the final resting place of Paul Gauguin, the French impressionist painter who came to live here in 1901 and, more recently, of the Belgian singer, Jacques Brel, who died there in 1978 having run Atuona's open-air cinema for several years.

Maupiti

Way out west in French Polynesia's Leeward Islands you come to the volcanic high island of Maupiti, a green postage stamp in the vast ocean with a surface area of just 11 sq km (4 sq mi), surrounded by long motu (islets) that enclose an immense shallow lagoon with just one access point for boats. Traditionally, Maupiti has strong cultural links with Bora Bora, 40 km (25 mi) to the east, and is sometimes described as 'Bora Bora's beautiful little cousin'.

WHEN TO GO:
Any time – this is a magical island for all seasons, even more spectacular in the summer rainy season (December to April) when clouds and sudden storms enhance the drama.

If you really want a get-away-from-it-all holiday, this is the place for you. There are no resorts and no organized tours – just a few simple guest-houses and rooms to rent in family homes. Remember to take cash, because there's no way of getting any unless the bank is open (which is an infrequent occurrence). The pace of life here is slow and peaceful, ensuring that the only viable options are to relax, relax and relax.

It takes but two hours to stroll around the island, enjoying dramatic scenery (Mount Hotu

Maupiti in the foreground, Bora Bora in the distance

A glorious sunset seen through the palm trees

Paraoa plunges straight into the sea at the island's southern tip) and wonderful sandy beaches (notably Tereia Beach at the western point). The main settlements of Farauru and Vaiea are on the eastern side. A three-hour hike takes you to the top of the

HOW TO GET THERE:
By twice-weekly boat from
Bora Bora (the Maupiti
Express) or thrice weekly by
air from Tahiti via Raiatea or
Bora Bora.

HIGHLIGHTS:
The tiny islet of Motu Paeao
on the north side of Maupiti,
where archaeologists found
graves and artefacts from
the earliest period of
Polynesian civilization.
Snorkelling around Onoiau
Pass – the only boat access
to the island.
Interesting petroglyphs
carved into rock at the
northern end of
the island.

YOU SHOULD KNOW:
After tourism, Maupiti's
chief economic activity is
growing noni (Indian or
beach mulberry), but don't
be tempted to scrump one –
an alternative name is
'vomit fruit'.

central peak of Mount Teurafaatui, and the reward is a
sensational panorama over the lagoon to Bora Bora
and (on a clear day) Raiatea and Tahaa. Maupiti is a
genuine South Sea island paradise.

129

Lord Howe Island

WHEN TO GO:
Cheapest to get there out of season but it can be wetter and windier and some places may be closed. From September to April huge numbers of exotic seabirds nest here.

HOW TO GET THERE:
By air from Sydney or Brisbane.

HIGHLIGHTS:
Sooty terns on the accessible summit of Mount Eliza (from August to March).
Ned's Beach – a daily fish feeding frenzy attracting reef sharks.
Ball's Pyramid – dive trips around the world's tallest stack, rising from the sea 23 km (14 mi) to the southeast.

YOU SHOULD KNOW:
Some rare mushrooms on the island glow in the dark. These glowing mushrooms appear after heavy rain in the palm forests. If picked they glow for a number of days. The glow is so bright that you can read by it in the dark.

Unpolluted and untouched, Lord Howe Island is the ultimate eco-destination. Back in Victorian times, stories came to England of this 'gem of the sea', and to this day over two-thirds of the land is given over to a park reserve and only 400 people can visit at any one time. Often the animals outnumber the people. There's only one road, and everyone tends to get around by bicycle, boat or on foot. Just 11 km (7 mi) long, this boomerang-shaped beauty is topped by the rainforest-clad Mount Gower and Mount Lidgbird and dips down into the cool Tasman Sea. Born of a volcanic eruption some seven million years ago, it has the southernmost coral reef in the world – safe haven for 500 species of fish and 90 species of corals.

Lord Howe Island was discovered in 1788 by Lieutenant Henry Lidgbird Ball of HMS *Supply*, while on his way from Botany Bay to Norfolk Island with convicts on board. Many government ships, whaling and trading vessels stopped here but a permanent settlement wasn't established until 1834, at an area now known as Old Settlement.

Nowadays, the locals are laidback and often barefoot, and set the tone for any visit. On the more popular northern end of the island, there are endless walks and lookouts, and ideal places for a picnic along Old Settlement Beach. Bushwalking apart, there are fabulous swimming, snorkelling and diving spots. This insanely beautiful island never appears crowded – and if it is, it's with exotic flora and fauna not human life.

NEXT: Lord Howe Island from the air

The view towards Mount Gower and Mount Lidgbird

Paddle Steamer on the Murray River

HOW:
By boat
WHEN TO GO:
All year
TIME IT TAKES:
Four nights for the round trip.
HIGHLIGHTS:
Watching the birds and animals by the riverbank in the early morning.
Taking a guided nocturnal tour to seek out the varied wildlife that emerges after dark.
The ancient rock carvings at Ngaut Ngaut Aboriginal Reserve.

The presence of Australia's principal river, the Murray, has been a key factor in turning the south east of the country into its most productive and heavily populated area. The American writer Mark Twain hailed the Murray as Australia's Mississippi, although in a country where water has always been a limited resource it lacks the flow of its mighty American counterpart. Like the Mississippi the Murray offered a means of navigation for the early European settlers to reach the rich pastoral country inland; and for over fifty years from the 1860s it reigned unchallenged as the main transport artery for the region, carrying livestock and produce downriver to the coast and bringing supplies back to the sheep and cattle stations.

As in America the paddle steamer was the dominant means of river transport in these years. Where once they had a strictly commercial, utilitarian role these elegant vessels now ply their trade on the Murray as leisure boats. There is no better way to enjoy the varied sights of this riverscape – the mighty cliff-faces, the stands of towering red gums, the wetlands with their abundant wildlife – than from the deck of a paddle steamer as you glide by in sedate comfort.

At the historic river port of Mannum, on the Murray's lower reaches and an hour's drive east of Adelaide, you board the *Murray Princess* for an extended cruise upriver to the first lock near Blanchetown and back again, sleeping on board in well-appointed cabins. The rewards for opting for this slower and gentler form of transport are many, not least the grandstand views it gives you of the river's spectacular birdlife – pelicans, black swans and egrets are all commonly seen here.

YOU SHOULD KNOW:
If you want to be independent and fancy something a little more exclusive you can rent your own houseboat to take out on the river.

The Murray Princess
near Swan Reach

135

OFF THE BEATEN TRACK
ESCAPES

Gotska Sandön

WHEN TO GO:
Late May to early
September unless you are a
serious endurance
enthusiast.
HOW TO GET THERE:
By boat from Nynäshamn on
the mainland or the island
of Faro
HIGHLIGHTS:
Gamla Gården – an old farm
where there are Viking
artefacts.
Tarnüdden – the beach on
the south coast.
Madame Souderland's
homestead – the 18th
century house of the first
woman to live on the island.
Borgström's – a fishing
cottage built out of
driftwood and shipwreckage
in 1900.
YOU SHOULD KNOW:
Visitor numbers are strictly
regulated and you have to
obtain a permit. You can
stay either in the camping
site, a simple cottage or
sleeping hut.

This giant sand dune is the most remote island in the Baltic – isolated in the middle of the sea 38 km (24 mi) to the north of Gotland. It is just 9 km (6 mi) long by 6 km (4 mi) across, part of the crest of an undersea ridge formed by glaciation, almost entirely composed of sand with a few odd areas of moraine and rocky beach. From a distance Gotska Sandön looks completely flat but when you walk around you soon realize how hilly sand dunes can be. The highest point is 42 m (138 ft) above sea level.

Despite its distance from the mainland, there are signs of human activity from the Stone Age onwards. It was used as a seal hunting and fishing base by the Faro islanders, who also grazed their sheep here, but there were no permanent inhabitants until the 18th century. From 1783-1859 the island was privately owned. It eventually became Swedish Crown territory and is now a National Park.

The island is mainly pine woods with ground cover of heather, cowberries (lingon) and moss. In places the forest is incredibly dense and contains many rare insects and plants. The entire coast is bordered

PREVIOUS: Travelling along the Magellan Strait, which separates Patagonia from Tierra del Fuego.

by a sand ridge 10-15 m (33-50 ft) high and 100-300 m (330-985 ft) wide where there are shifting sand dunes which move up to 6 m (20 ft) a year.

There is no harbour so landing is a tricky exercise – leaping straight from the ferry onto the shore or, in bad weather, beaching by rubber dinghy. There are few concessions to the 21st century on Gotska Sandön: it is perfectly possible to be stranded for several days, the only transport on the entire island is a single tractor, there are no shops or restaurants, and hardly any inhabitants. If you want an adventure in self-sufficiency this is the place to come.

The beaches are bordered by deceptively tall sand dunes.

Dartmoor

WHAT IS IT:
Southern England's greatest
expanse of wilderness
HOW TO GET THERE:
From London it is a 281 km
(174 mi) journey west to
Exeter at the northeastern
edge of the moor. Trains run
regularly from London
(Paddington).
WHEN TO GO:
Any time of year is good,
but November to February
is especially atmospheric.
NEAREST TOWN:
Tavistock is the largest of
Dartmoor's towns.

*The medieval Clapper
Bridge in Postbridge*

Sprawling across Devon, in south west England,
between the towns of Plymouth and Exeter, Dartmoor
is as starkly beautiful as it is historically fascinating.
Occupying 4,700 hectares (11,610 acres) of desolate
wilderness: heather-strewn moors, barren bog land and
mile upon mile of raw granite, this is the place to come
for a sense of Nature at her most stoical.

At its centre is Dartmoor Forest where you can find
the famous wild ponies, ancient weather-chiselled tors
(flat granite hilltops), and, if you catch the right
weather, you will see the mist coming down, imbuing
this desolate terrain with a bleak and magical beauty.
But be warned, it is easy to lose your way and
bottomless bogs and stinking mires are never far away.

Dartmoor was once home to many Bronze Age
settlers whose artefacts can be viewed all over the
area, particularly to the east at Grimspound. Man's

more recent contribution comes in the form of Dartmoor Prison, in Princetown, originally built for the POWs captured in the Napoleonic Wars. And, at nearby Wistman's Wood, it is not hard to picture the druid gatherings that are thought to have taken place amongst the gnarled old trees.

In literature, it is Sir Arthur Conan Doyle who captured the spirit of Dartmoor best with his grimly transfixing *The Hound of the Baskervilles*. Within its pages the reader can absorb the dark tales and sinister myths that linger on the Moor. 'So vast and so mysterious,' he mused. The tumbling streams in the forest, the trout that swim under Fingle Bridge, the solitary kestrels and the crazed buzzards circling overhead; all against the grim presence of the prison and the endless, beguiling view from the heights of High Willhays. There is the creeping possibility that maybe, if you get in too deep, you might become lost here forever.

Colourful heather below Haytor Rocks, a 454 m (1,489 ft) granite tor

NEXT: The Dartmoor scenery is shaped by its unpredictable weather.

The Dingle Peninsula

WHAT IS IT:
The most westerly point of Ireland

HOW TO GET THERE:
By road

WHEN TO GO:
Summer but pack a raincoat!

NEAREST TOWN:
Dingle

YOU SHOULD KNOW:
The drive from Dingle over the Connor Pass is not for the fainthearted.

The northernmost of the five peninsulas that project out into the Atlantic like fingers at the south-west tip of Ireland, the Dingle Peninsula (Corca Dhuibhne) is the westernmost point of mainland Ireland. It lies on a sandstone ridge that also forms the Slieve Mish mountains in the east of the peninsula and Mount Brandon, Ireland's second highest mountain at 953 m (3,127 ft).

Often beset by the weather that the North Atlantic throws at it, this wild landscape is known for its spectacular scenery with stunning views of Great Blasket Island, Dingle Bay and across Castlemaine Harbour to MacGillicuddy Reeks. Described by many as one of the most beautiful landscapes on Earth, it has rocky outcrops and rugged cliffs, soft rounded hills with forests, beautiful alpine-arctic flora higher up and wide sandy beaches. There is a magnificent view around almost every corner. Off the beaten track, there are many side roads and paths that allow visitors to explore this breathtaking countryside at their leisure.

In spring and early summer, seabirds such as gannets nest on the cliffs. Popular activities include walking, boat trips to Great Blasket Island, swimming, surfing, walking or horse-riding through the edge of the surf. There are also hundreds of archaeological sites to visit.

A traditional cottage near Dunquinn

Cape Clear Island

WHEN TO GO:
June to September for
festivities, April, May and
October for tranquillity and
bird watching.
HOW TO GET THERE:
By ferry from Baltimore on
the mainland, all year round.
HIGHLIGHTS:
Spotting dolphins, whales,
leatherback turtles, sunfish
and basking shark in the
surrounding waters.
The Old Lighthouse.
Learn a little more history
by visiting the Cape Clear
Museum.
Admire the surreally
beautiful wind turbines.
Dive, windsurf, sail, canoe
and fish off the island.
Enjoy the *craic* of an
evening in one of the
island's pubs.
YOU SHOULD KNOW:
The first weekend of
September is the time for
Cape Clear's International
Storytelling Festival, when
professional storytellers
from around the world keep
you spellbound for hours.

Cape Clear Island is an absolute gem, deserving of all the superlatives you can think of, the pot of gold at the end of the rainbow. Only 5 km (3 mi) long by 2 km (1.5 mi) wide, it is Ireland's most southerly inhabited point, and because of its position, its climate is more benign than that of the mainland.

Cape Clear is one of Ireland's last remaining *gaeltacht* (Irish language speaking) islands, and during the summer months the small, permanent population swells considerably with an influx of students, anxious to brush up their language skills. This was the birthplace of St Ciaran, supposedly the earliest of Ireland's pre-Patrician saints, and the ruins of his 12th century church stands near the harbour.

The island has several ancient remains, including Megalithic standing stones and a 5,000 year-old passage grave. The ruin of the 14th century O'Driscoll Castle stills hugs its headland overlooking the harbour, which is the island's commercial centre. The castle itself is very hard to reach, a feat only to be attempted on a fine weather day.

Cape Clear's physical position off the coast of County Cork puts it firmly in the path of thousands of migrating birds – indeed it is one of the country's foremost bird-watching sites. As long ago as 1959 an Observatory was established near the harbour,

manned by enthusiastic, knowledgeable ornithologists.

This is a hilly, fertile place, with soaring cliffs, gentle hills, bogs, a reed swamp, a lake, lovely beaches, remote coves, heathland and farmland – just the ticket, in other words. Undeveloped and unspoilt, heather and gorse cover the hills, which in spring and summer are bright with wild flowers, while in autumn the bracken turns a deep russet red, lending a rich, mellow glow. Winter brings fierce gales, and the locals amuse themselves with storytelling and musical evenings around roaring fires.

*South Harbour on Cape
Clear Island*

147

A Coruña to Madrid

Considering how long Spain has been a major tourist destination, its magnificent hinterland has remained remarkably undiscovered. There is no better way to see the interior of this beautiful country than catching the train from the lovely city of A Coruña, on the Galician coast, to Madrid – a 740-km (460-mi) scenic journey that takes you through a sparsely populated rural backwater of historic hill villages and ancient agricultural landscapes with breathtaking views.

Leaving the dramatic coastal cliffs and bays of A Coruña behind, the train travels through the lush valleys and verdant woodlands of Galicia, up to the desolate romantic moorland around the city of Ourense on the banks of the River Miño, and through the virtually uninhabited borderlands of Spain and Portugal towards Zamora, across a mountain wilderness of rugged heath and forest where wolves still roam. Passing through countless tunnels, you cannot help thinking about the forced labour that built this section of the railway – half-starved Republican political prisoners of the 1940s and 50s, hacking their way through the mountain rock in pitch-darkness.

From Zamora, known as a 'museum of Romanesque art' for its 12th- and 13th-century churches, the railway meanders through the vineyards of the fertile Duero Valley and cuts across the ancient farmlands of the Tierra del Campo. The last leg takes you up past olive and citrus groves, oak and pine forests into the highlands north of Madrid. Finally you descend to the plain of Castilla y León and arrive at Spain's impressive capital city; by now your head will be full of splendid scenic impressions and you will already be planning to explore more deeply into this world away from the usual hackneyed tourist itineraries.

HOW:
By train
WHEN TO GO:
April to October
TIME IT TAKES:
Ten hours minimum
HIGHLIGHTS:
Tower of Hercules, A Coruña – the oldest lighthouse in the world, dating from the 2nd century with magnificent views from the top.
Scenic mountain landscape between Ourense and Zamora
The Duero Valley
The Castle of Medina del Campo
YOU SHOULD KNOW:
If you have the time, this journey is interesting to do in stages, stopping off at Ourense and Zamora on your way.

NEXT: The Tower of Hercules lighthouse, A Coruña

Detail of the sacrifice of Isaac by Abraham, Church of Saint Peter of the Ship, Zamora

149

Trevelez, possibly the highest mountain village in Spain

The White Villages of La Alpujarra

After the official expulsion of the Moors from Spain in 1492, refugees retreated into La Alpujarra, an inaccessible region of steep valleys in the southern Sierra Nevada, where they survived in isolated pockets for a further 150 years by cultivating the fertile silt

washed down from the mountains. Today some 70 'white villages' are testimony to the Moorish cultural roots of the inhabitants. On a hike through this beautiful rugged country the Moroccan Berber influence can be seen all around – in the inimitable terracing of the fields, intricate irrigation techniques and cubic architecture.

The land is so steep that the quaint whitewashed houses with flat roofs and crooked clay chimneys seem to be piled on top of each other, each village an idiosyncratic jumble of narrow streets. The beautifully tended terraces of olive, fig, mulberry and nut trees are constantly watered by melting snow, directed down the mountains along *acequias* (irrigation channels). A network of ancient walled trails and mule paths takes you along ridges dotted with cacti, down into rocky wooded gorges, through almond groves and wildflower meadows, always with breathtaking views of the snowy peaks of the Sierra Nevada.

From Mairena, a typically picturesque white village, you head westwards to the charming village of Yegen, leaning precariously on a narrow ledge. The twisting

HOW:
On foot
WHEN TO GO:
March to May for the wild flowers or September to October for the autumn colour.
TIME IT TAKES:
Six to seven days
HIGHLIGHTS:
Moorish cubic architecture. Outstanding natural scenery. Trevélez – highest town in Spain with a church at 1,476 m (4,840 ft). Yegen – village made famous in the 1920s and 30s by the Hispanophile English writer Gerald Brenan, a friend of Virginia Woolf who came here to stay with him.
YOU SHOULD KNOW:
This is a moderately easy trek for anyone reasonably fit. La Alpujarra is excellent walking country, crisscrossed by trails of varying difficulty, but can equally well be toured by car, bike or horse.

trail leads through several hamlets up to the pretty village of Mecina Bombaron and then across ridge and river to Bérchules in the high mountain grasslands. A steep descent through pine forest followed by another climb through flower-filled meadows takes you to your destination – the village of Trevélez.

Toppling over a frighteningly steep gorge, it is arguably the highest village in Spain. Here you can reward yourself for your long trek with what is indisputably the best-tasting Serrano ham in the country.

A typical courtyard in La Alpujarra

Giannutri

The smallest and most southerly inhabited island of the Tuscan Archipelago, Giannutri is a half moon of just 3 sq km (1.16 sq mi). From the sea it appears inaccessible, even forbidding; but the black volcanic boulders that form an unbroken barrier around it are more blessing than bane.

Centuries of shifting rock falls have made it one of the finest diving sites in the Mediterranean, with no sand to cloud the lapis waters; and since there are no beaches at all to attract conventional tourism, the circlet of rocks has preserved the island's wild beauty from all modern depredations.

Patrician Romans loved it. They built the small port, and dotted their villas among the vines, olive trees

The ruins of Villa
Domizia on Giannutri

WHEN TO GO:
May to September
HOW TO GET THERE:
By ferry from Porto Santo
Stéfano on Argentario
HIGHLIGHTS:
The Roman seaside Villa
Domizia.
The lighthouse at Punto
Rosso, built in 1861.
The rare Mediterranean
corals and underwater
meadows of the Marine
Park.
YOU SHOULD KNOW:
The exact zoning of the
Marine Park; there are
heavy fines for breaking the
rules.

and myriad wild flowers of the interior. Long abandoned, one of them was restored in the late 19th century by one of Garibaldi's naval captains, Gualtiero Adami. He cultivated some of the land, becoming known as Giannutri's own Robinson Crusoe. Local legend has it that the wind is the howling of his lover, Marietta, perpetually desolate after his death in 1922.

There are no cars, and few people. You walk in the cacophonous 'silence' of the purely natural world, senses sharpened by intense colours and heady perfumes of herb and flower. Offshore it gets even better. Dolphins, turtles and sea horses patrol huge meadows of ravishing underwater Poseidonia, set with waving sea fans of coral and sea roses. Ghosts of 2,000 year-old wrecks are shrouded in fronds and guarded by darting fish. Large areas of the Marine Park are set aside for swimming and diving, to the exclusion of boats either in transit or moored, and of fishing. You can do those in many other places. Giannutri's utopian charm provides an opportunity to escape all forms of modern hurly-burly, on land or underwater.

The Plitvice Lakes

Waterfalls connect the upper and lower sections of the lakes.

In the heart of the forbidding forests of Croatia's Dinaric Mountains – marked on old maps as 'The Devil's Garden' – there is an enchanting valley. Here is one of the most outstanding natural wonders in Europe – the Plitvice Lakes.

   These are sixteen interconnected naturally terraced

157

WHAT IS IT:
A group of 16 interconnected lakes
HOW TO GET THERE:
Fly to Zagreb. Road from Zagreb to Dalmatia 140 km (88 mi)
WHEN TO GO:
Anytime
NEAREST TOWN:
Slunj 35 km (22 mi)
DON'T MISS:
Barac's Caves 6 km (4 mi) east of Rakovika near the village of Nova Krslja
YOU SHOULD KNOW:
The forest around the Plitvice Lakes was a central theatre in the Croatian War of Independence. Soldiers from both sides took up positions in the caves and mined the forest. One of the first priorities of the new government was to clear the Lakes and surrounding woods of unexploded munitions.

lakes. At each terrace, water gushes out through hundreds of holes in the porous wall as well as spilling over the lip, cascading into the lake below in never-ending streams of sparkling clear water. The exquisite colours of the lakes – azures, blues and greens – are constantly changing according to the sunlight and the quantity of mineral deposits in the water.

The terraces are made from travertine – a weird rock-like substance composed of limestone sediment (deposited by the mountain streams) mixed with algae and mosses. The travertine builds up in layers around the vegetation, petrifying it and creating bizarre shapes as it hardens. At Plitvice, the travertine has built up so thickly it has formed natural dams, which have led to the creation of the lakes.

The lakes are in two separate clusters, extending over 8 km (5 mi), and covering an area of 2 sq km (¾ sq mi). The upper part of the valley contains twelve lakes, ending in Veliki Slap (Big Waterfall), a dramatic waterfall that spills over a sharp drop into a sheer canyon 70 m (230 ft) below. This canyon contains four more lakes, which finally become the River Korana.

The beauty of the lakes is breathtaking at any time of year. The forest is blanketed in snow in winter and has long hot Mediterranean summers. It supports an exceptional diversity of plants and wildlife, harbouring deer, wild boars, wolves and bears. It is reputed to be the most beautiful spot in Europe and is a World Heritage Site.

The lower falls at Plitvice Lakes

The Golden Mountains of Altai

WHAT IS IT:
The high mountain wilderness of southern Siberia
HOW TO GET THERE:
Bus from Barnaul to Artybash (Altaisky) or Tyungur (Katunsky)
WHEN TO GO:
May to August

Wild and majestic, the Altai range marks the junction of Central Asia and Siberia, and of Russia with China, Mongolia and Kazakhstan. It's the heartland of Russia's most ancient cultures; but the standing stones and sacred sites of the Altai and Scythian peoples have all but been reclaimed by wilderness. Colossal tracts have now been set aside as Reserves to protect the mosaic of eco-systems that underwrites the region's grandeur and variety. Just one of them, the Altaisky Nature

Reserve, has a core area of 881,200 hectares (2.2 million acres), which includes every permutation of steppe, taiga, alpine meadow, highland forest, glacial lake, mountain tundra and snow-capped peak, and at every level, the richest diversity of appropriate fauna and flora, and some of the rarest. The Altaisky also contains the 'Jewel of Western Siberia', Lake Teletskoye. It is 78 km (49 mi) long, a sky-blue ribbon only 5 km (3 mi) wide, snaking between cragged peaks and imperial stands of Siberian cedar forest.

Fed by 70 rivers and 150 melt water cascades, its crystal water is among the purest on earth; when wind-shadows refract the huge skies, snowy peaks and

NEAREST TOWN:
Gorno-Altaisk 500 km
(312 mi)
DON'T MISS:
Lake Teletskoye
YOU SHOULD KNOW:
The snow leopard does not roar.

Yurts in the foothills of the Altai Mountains

A snow leopard

swaying forest green reflected on its surface, it is said to re-define beauty.

The Katunsky Reserve holds a cross-section of Altai's natural treasures – 148 separate glaciers within 80 sq km (31 sq mi) feed the mighty Katun River, overlooked by Mt. Belukha, Siberia's highest at 4,136 m (13,600 ft). Every step opens a new panorama of crags, forest, lakes and high meadows carpeted with wild flowers; and the nearby Multa lakes, descending the high ridges in a series of 30-70 m (98-230 ft) waterfalls, are the particular home of bear, ibex and snow leopard. Eventually, the wild Katun gorge opens onto pastures among gentle alps, broadens, and unites with other mountain rivers to become the great Siberian River Ob.

Wadi Rum

Wadi Rum is quite simply one of the most astonishingly, austerely beautiful places in the world. It fulfils every romantic notion of a desert landscape, complete with sheer, dark granite mountains, sandstone ridges rising vertically from the pink sand of the desert floor, and ancient graffiti scratched on the rocks of these vast and silent valleys.

Man has inhabited this place from Neolithic times, and the presence of freshwater springs made it a natural meeting place for caravans wending their way across the desert. In the 1st century BC, the Nabataeans settled here, before decamping to the rose coloured city of Petra. Everyone left their mark in the form of Neolithic flint axes, ironage pottery, cave paintings and a Nabataean temple.

Jabal Rum is the highest peak here at 1,754 m (5,315 ft). On a clear day, rock climbers can see both the Saudi Arabian border and the Red Sea from the summit. In early spring, after the rains, the desert explodes with life. Wildflowers colour the landscape – red anemones, black iris, bright poppies and medicinal herbs abound. Eagles and buzzards wheel and drift in

WHAT IS IT:
One of the most amazing desertscapes in the world
HOW TO GET THERE:
By road from Aqaba or Petra
WHEN TO GO:
March, April, September, October and November
NEAREST TOWN:
Wadi Rum village 6 km (3.75 mi) Rashidiya 30 km (18.75 mi)
DON'T MISS:
The Seven Pillars of Wisdom mountain
YOU SHOULD KNOW:
Wadi Rum was the headquarters of the legendary T.E. Lawrence, who named the mountain; much of the film *Lawrence of Arabia* was shot here.

The entrance to a valley at Wadi Rum

163

the sky above, just two of the 110 bird species recorded here. Ibex, grey wolves, Arabian sand cats and foxes all thrive in this region. Nomadic Bedouin still graze their herds, judging when to pack up and move on.

This is a protected environment: before entering Wadi Rum you will find the fort of the famous Desert Patrol, who police the area astride camels, wearing flowing robes and red and white headdresses, daggers at their waists and rifles across their backs. Rest under the vast, star spangled night sky sipping a cardamom coffee, and listen to the sound of silence.

Sandstone formations at Wadi Rum

Jiuhuashan Trek

*The Zhiyuan temple
at Jiuhuashan*

Of China's four Buddhist sacred mountains, Jiuhuashan
represents the South. Its temples are dedicated to
Bodhisatva Ksitigarbha, lord of the earth and
underworld. It rises on the northern edge of the Yangtze
flood plains in Anhui Province, west of Shanghai. Above
the glassy terraces of rice paddy, the road climbs into
ragged pine forests, twisting deep into a landscape of
forest-capped cliffs, cascades and massive, bizarre rock
formations. In the mist creeping up from the valleys,
shapes form in the washed-out colours of ancient

HOW:
On foot
WHEN TO GO:
Year-round. Each season has
its adherents – for example
the Taoyan Waterfall, on
Jiuhuashan's north side, is at
its best after seasonal rain,
when the river's force
creates an all-pervading
misty haze.

165

TIME IT TAKES:
2-4 days (to get any real sense of it), though a number of agencies bring visitors for a day's excursion.

HIGHLIGHTS:
The Precious Hall of the Bodhisattva Incarnate, on Shenguang Ridge near the Huachengsi Monastery – a scarlet, 7-storey wooden pagoda with over 100 'incarnation' statues of Kim Kiao Kak, the Korean monk who achieved nirvana and brought fame to Jiuhuashan as incarnation of the Hell-King.

The Sea of Bamboo at Minyuan – in a breeze, 405 hectares (1,000 acres) of tall bamboo 'sings' to the gurgling springs and bubbling streams beside the mountain path.

The Phoenix Pine, aka. 'No.1 Pine in the Land Under Heaven' – planted 1,400 years ago, the flat crown of its foliage resembles a green phoenix craning its neck towards Tiantai ('Heavenly Terrace'), at 1,325 m (4,346 ft), one of Jiuhuashan's most important peaks.

Chinese paintings, and you feel a déja-vu familiarity. Though there are tea and vegetable plantations among the blossoming azaleas, these are cultivated by the monks and nuns of some 80 temples and sacred institutions, and they don't impinge on the otherwise authentic wilderness. But more than 1,500 years of sanctity means that Jiuhuashan's nine principal peaks, and every cave, stream, path, promontory, pool, waterfall, cliff, temple, pagoda and even the 'Ten Perfect Views', have names of meditational significance (like 'Celestial Presence at the Heavenly Pillar') – which transforms hiking on the mountain into an involuntary pilgrimage whenever genuine pilgrims pause on the often narrow path.

It's no hardship. The goodwill you encounter trekking on Jiuhuashan enhances what is already an exceptionally lovely region. There is no development other than the stunning temple complexes, all of them integrated into the dramatic landscape according to the principles of the Tang, Ming and Qing dynasties in which they were built. You choose temple guesthouses over campsites, and seek out some of their 1,500 Buddha statues and thousands of important cultural relics – because rapidly you realize how their existence gives meaning to every rock and tree that you might hike past. With wafting incense, temple bells and a shrine on every corner, this is not normal hiking – but Jiuhuashan's natural magnificence and spiritual integrity make it abnormally rewarding.

Monasteries cling to the mountainside.

Wat Tham Pha

WHAT IS THERE TO SEE:
The Dao Caves, the Elephant Training Centre at Taeng-Dao and Chiang Mai
HOW DO I GET THERE:
You can only travel here by road.
YOU SHOULD KNOW:
There is an entrance fee.

A view of the jungle from the look-out point

Situated in the mountains above Chiang Dao stands one of the most beautiful temples in Thailand. Virtually unknown to tourists, it is sufficiently remote as to be visited hardly at all, and yet it is a working monastery with a serene and spiritual atmosphere. Made from stone, with a gilded stupa, the temple sits easily with its surroundings, and its simplicity comes as a relief after the scores of painted and glittering temples you will have already seen.

To reach the temple you must climb a pathway that meanders up and through the forest. Surrounded by

A small shrine near the temple

tall trees and with bougainvillea and frangipani tumbling down the rocky outcrops, it is some time before you catch a glimpse of the lovely mountain Wat perched way above you. The only sound to break the silence is birdsong, and the only people to be seen are monks sweeping the leaves from the path and steps. At about the half-way point is a look-out spot with excellent views, but it is not until you have reached the temple itself, with its shrine dug out of the rock face, that you realize how high you are, and find that the view from the top is not just beautiful, it is absolutely spectacular.

Jobo Mountain Adventure Drive

HOW:
On foot, by 4x4 or on horseback

WHEN TO GO:
October, November, March to May

TIME IT TAKES:
Pony treks last from a few hours to three days; 4x4 treks last as long as you like.

HIGHLIGHTS:
Getting to know the friendly, cheerful Basuto people.
Basuto huts: many of the one-roomed huts (*rondavels*) are decorated with intricate, symbolic murals.
The Sani rock paintings, deep in a sheltering cave, are well preserved.
The view from Jobo Mountain is sensational.

YOU SHOULD KNOW:
Some 4x4 routes should only be attempted by experienced off-road drivers.
Each summer several people die from lightning strikes, so avoid high, open ground during storms.

Lesotho – the 'Kingdom of the Sky' – is a small, mountainous country surrounded by South Africa. Though British rule was resented in the 19th century, this British Protectorate (Basutoland) was not included in the Union of South Africa, and the peaceful kingdom avoided the long years of apartheid.

Rural Lesotho is perfect trekking country. Dominated by mountain ranges, this is a land without fences where herd-boys drive their flocks and blanket-wrapped farmers ride. In the south, a relatively small area around the village of Malealea seems to offer all the best features of the highlands. Here are precipitous mountains and gorges, ancient rock paintings, waterfalls and a scattering of remote villages fluttering with bright flags. These flags are colour-coded advertisements for the available comestibles – red and green for meat and vegetables,

white and yellow for sorghum or barley beer.

Fittingly, this area is reached through the Gates of Paradise Pass. The lodge here will advise on routes for walkers and drivers of 4x4s and arrange pony treks. Ponies and guides are provided by the villages, and longer treks spend nights in village huts. The Basuto are a nation of horsemen and their small,

Traditional Basuto huts

*A view towards the
Maluti Mountains*

strong, surefooted ponies are the ideal form of transport. No wild gallops here, though: the ponies pick their way carefully up and down the steep tracks. Very gentle, they are ideal for non-riders.

A trek to Jobo Mountain and village is one of the most rewarding and exciting journeys. The route covers the Sani rock paintings and the Botso'ela Waterfall and the final climb is along a precarious pass between two beautiful, deep gorges. Most 4x4 drivers prefer to walk the last, vertiginous section.

Raft Cove

On the north-west coast of Vancouver Island is Cape Scott Park. At the southern end of the park you will discover Raft Cove, a provincial park consisting of an isolated, forested coastline at the mouth of the meandering Macjack River.

Cutting through an unpaved, twisting trail, among ancient towering hemlock, western red cedar and Sitka spruce, you will come upon the rugged shoreline, notable for its unobstructed majestic views of the pounding Pacific. From here you might be lucky enough to see migrating whales. At the end of the beach is a wild sandy bay, accessible at low tide, which is home to the dilapidated trapper's cabin of Willie Hecht, an early Cape Scott settler. Abandoned and crumbling, the remnants of Hecht's home lie on the southern bank, opposite the tip of the wooded peninsula. The best fresh water is available from the nearby stream.

Camping on the beach, or in wilderness campsites amongst the canopy of trees, is popular as are surfing, swimming, fishing and hiking. Black bears, cougars and wolves live in the park so caution should be exercised when staying overnight. This is the land of pioneers, virtually untouched by man. Hiking here, you will feel as though you are discovering your own secret wilderness.

WHAT IS IT:
A provincial park known for its solitude and rugged coastline
WHERE IS IT:
On the north-west of Vancouver Island
WHAT IS THERE TO DO:
Camp, fish, hike, kayak or just enjoy the scenery
YOU SHOULD KNOW:
Dress warmly and bring good rain gear at any time of the year, as Raft Cove is very exposed to the Pacific weather systems that pound this rugged coastline.

A beautiful sunset at Raft Cove

Baffin Island

WHEN TO GO:
June to August
HOW TO GET THERE:
By air from Montreal,
Ottawa or Yellowknife
HIGHLIGHTS:
Kimmirut – famous for its
aboriginal stone-carving
industry.
Auyuittuq National Park: a
pristine wilderness within
the Arctic Circle.
Pond Inlet: a stunning mix of
mountains, icebergs and
glaciers.
The Pangnirtung Pass – a
spectacular 100 km (62 mi)
hike around fjords
YOU SHOULD KNOW:
In the summer the
inhabitants of Iqaluit leave
their homes to live in tents
and visitors are invited too.
There is no better way to
plan a trip than to sit around
a campfire, under the
midnight sun and discuss it
with the people who know
the landscape best.

Baffin Island is in the eastern Canadian Arctic, lying between Greenland and the Canadian mainland. Covering 507,451 sq km (195,928 sq mi), it is the largest island in North America and the fifth largest in the world. It was named after the British explorer William Baffin but the overwhelmingly Inuit population know it as Qikiqtaaluk.

Made up of a dozen or so sparsely populated

communities, Baffin lives up to its reputation for being unspoiled, untamed and undiscovered. With sixty per cent of the island lying above the Arctic Circle and summer temperatures struggling to reach even 5° C (41° F), this rugged ice-covered landscape is not for the fainthearted. However the rewards for any visitor are great, with unrivalled scenery and the chance to see the rich and diverse Arctic wildlife, including polar bears and whales, in their natural environment.

Baffin Island, unspoiled and untamed

Getting to Baffin Island is only feasible by air. The island has only one airport (Iqaluit) which deals with external flights and another six which handle internal transfers. Arriving at Iqaluit you will find a thriving First Nations community. This capital of the newly-formed state of Nunavut can provide all you need for a kayaking, canoeing or trekking holiday.

Most of the finest mountains are located on the Cumberland Peninsula, at the head of the South Pangnirtung Fjord. Much of the area is included within Auyuittuq National Park, and is accessible from Pangnirtung, a small coastal Inuit settlement. Access to the peaks is by boat, dog sled, float-plane or ski-plane, depending on ice and weather conditions.

The sheer vastness of the island is difficult to take in and any traveller should plan ahead, not be too ambitious and allow extra time for weather-related delays, even in summer.

The town of Iqaluit

Rio Grande

Big Bend National Park in Texas is like the state itself
– larger than life and many countries. This vast area is
bounded by the Rio Grande to the south, which forms
the border with Mexico, and the Park is a land of
extremes – from desert to mountain, majestic rivers
to inaccessible wilderness. The variety of plants and
wildlife – especially birds – is extraordinary, and the
Park's facilities are often stretched during high season
(cooler winter
months). But there's

*Taking a break
from rafting.*

one way of getting
round that problem –
taking to the water,
to kayak through the
Chihuahuan Desert
with open views and
a dramatic river-
scape that includes
canyons up to 460 m
(1,500 ft) deep.

The Rio Grande
runs for 190 km
(118 mi) within the
Park, and a further
205 km (127 mi)
downstream is
designated a Wild and
Scenic River. There is
plenty of calm water,
but this is not a
journey for beginners
as there are periodic
encounters with
rapids of varying
severity, especially
when the water is

Cacti overlooking the river.

high. Unfortunately, extraction means it often isn't. The preferred option for experienced paddlers is a one- or two-person inflatable kayak, and even then this magnificent river is so remote that most people travel with a guide or organized party. It is possible to use your own equipment or hire locally (though not in the Park). Permits are required for self-organized trips, allowing you to stop off and explore interesting

HOW:
By kayak
DEPART:
Lajitas, TX
WHEN TO GO:
November to April
TIME IT TAKES:
Lajitas to La Linda takes 10-
14 days, depending on stops
and side-trips
HIGHLIGHTS:
The beautiful journey
through popular Santa Elena
Canyon – great scenery,
serenity...and the
excitement of the Rockslide
Rapids.
Sunset over Mexico's
remote Sierra del Carmen
(Carmen Mountains), south
of the river.
Marsical Canyon, the most
remote in Big Bend National
Park – just 16 km (10 mi)
long but with varied
scenery, towering limestone
cliffs, some rapids and
ample stop-off points along
the canyon bottom.
Rio Grande Village – one of
the few places along the
river that has all the
facilities.
YOU SHOULD KNOW:
Always camp on the US
bank and carry identity
documents – the Border
Patrol can show up at any
time and needs to know
you're not an 'illegal'.

side canyons.

To run the Rio Grande through the Park, start at
Lajitas on Texas Highway 170. Be aware that there are
few facilities and a limited number of take-outs along
the route and plan accordingly. Unless you intend to
run the full length of the Wild and Scenic section, you
end this unique journey at the Highway 2627 bridge in
La Linda. This is a 200-km (125-mi) trip.

El Yunque

HOW TO GET THERE:
There is no public transport to El Yunque, but Highway 191 (off Highway 3 from San Juan) runs right into the forest.
WHEN TO GO:
April to June are quiet months in the forest; in the hot summers, islanders flock there to cool down; winter (high season) can be hectic.
DON'T MISS:
A night in the rainforest. Camping is permitted off-trail, but it is very basic. Several hotels around the forest perimeter provide an enticing combination of comfort with the unforgettable music of the creatures of dusk and darkness.

Sometimes the rich Taino, European and African heritage of Puerto Rico seems overshadowed by modern American life, but the island probably owes the survival of its rainforests and rich biodiversity to US colonial rule. Logging and rapid urban expansion resulted in serious deforestation and soil erosion, but in the 1920s extensive areas of conservation forest were set aside and now thousands of tropical plant, bird and animal species flourish in a variety of natural habitats.

Much of eastern Puerto Rico is covered by the forests, hills, streams and waterfalls of El Yunque (previously known as the Caribbean National Forest), the only tropical rainforest under US administration. Now a UNESCO Biosphere Reserve, it is carefully managed and has hiking trails and visitor and research centres. A range of forest types grows here, including most of Puerto Rico's ancient virgin forest – many of

the reddish-barked Palo Colorado trees, with their trailing vines, are around 1,000 years old. Sierra palms, ferns and mosses thrive in wetter conditions and, on peaks and ridges, heavy rain and constant winds bend and stunt the cloud, or dwarf, forest. This sumptuously diverse landscape supports a wealth of wildlife. Although the endangered Puerto Rican parrot (which nests in the Palo Colorado trees) is rarely seen, more than 50 bird species, many unique, inhabit the reserve. Resident reptiles include the Puerto Rican boa.

Some of the shorter, paved trails to popular destinations (waterfalls, viewing towers and peaks) can get busy, but longer wilderness trails in the undeveloped south of the forest are often deserted. Serious walkers may leave the crowds behind and relish the cool, pristine beauty of this mountainous subtropical rainforest.

YOU SHOULD KNOW:
Do not attempt the longer trails without a good map and compass as it is easy to get lost in a rainforest. It rains, so take suitable clothing.

LEFT: A rainforest trail in El Yunque

ABOVE: A forest waterfall

Andes Cordillera

WHAT IS IT:
A mountain range
HOW TO GET THERE:
Fly to Lima or Cuzco
WHEN TO GO:
Year round but June to
August is best because it is
the dry season in the
highlands.
DON'T MISS:
Nevado Huaracán
Machu Picchu
Lake Titicaca
YOU SHOULD KNOW:
It takes time to acclimatize
to the altitudes here so you
should make your travel
plans accordingly.

*The Pyramid of
Garcilaso rises to
5885 m (19,307 ft)*

The Andes Cordillera is the longest continuous
mountain chain on earth and the highest outside Asia.
It extends more than 7,000 km (4,000 mi), running
through seven South American countries from
Tierra del Fuego to Venezuela. At its widest, the
range is 500 km (300 mi) across with an average
height of 4,000 m (13,000 ft). The mountains are
largely composed of limestone, sandstone, slate and
some granite, with large amounts of lava in the
volcanic regions.

Frequent earthquakes attest to the dynamic nature
of these awesome mountains. The Central Andes runs
down the whole length of Peru, home to some of the
most spectacular mountains in the world – steep
granite peaks rise above icy ridges with huge glaciers
snaking down the valleys to provide some of the most
magnificent landscapes you will ever come across.

The Pacific coast is never more than 160 km

(100 mi) away making for incredibly fast short rivers – a source of energy for the whole country. To the east, the glaciers feed the headwaters of the Amazon.

The Peruvian Andes are divided into five sub-ranges: Cordilleras Blanca and Huayhuash in the north, Central, Occidental and Oriental Cordilleras. Cordillera Blanca is by far the most accessible with the highest mountain in Peru, Nevada Huaracán. The Cordillera Occidental is an actively volcanic, more remote range in extreme southwest Peru, with mountains that are significantly easier to climb. The Oriental, in the region around Cuzco, the ancient capital of the Incan empire, is composed of several small ranges and isolated massifs, including Urubamba, the location of the famous abandoned Inca city of Machu Picchu. The southernmost range of the Oriental Cordillera, extending into Bolivia, is the remote and extremely glaciated Apolobamba. Its isolation gives it a unique quality and it is well worth exploring.

Lake Churup, 4,000 m (14,000 ft) up in the Cordillera Blanca mountains

NEXT: Part of the Sacred Valley, near Chincheros

The Atacama Desert

WHAT IS IT:
A mountainous desert
HOW TO GET THERE:
International flight to
Santiago. Domestic flight to
Calama 100 km (62 mi) away
then a shuttle flight /road to
San Pedro.
WHEN TO GO:
Avoid September to
November when winds reach
up to 100 kph (62 mph).
NEAREST TOWN:
San Pedro
DON'T MISS:
Chaxa Lagoon Reserva
Nacional Los Flamencos – a
flamingo breeding ground

*RIGHT: Two mountain
bikers survey the vast
landscape.*

*Chaxa Lagoon Reserva
Nacional Los Flamencos*

At its centre, the Atacama Desert is the driest place on earth – fifty times drier than California's Death Valley. The average annual rainfall is a mere 1 mm (0.004 in) and some parts never see any rain at all. The desert is at an altitude of over 2,000 m (6,560 ft), on a narrow plateau, only 150 km (94 mi) wide, which extends 1,000 km (625 mi) from the border with Peru into northern Chile. The rain shadow cast by the Andes on one side and the Pacific coastal mountains on the other has created an extraordinary landscape of alluvial saltpans. Incredibly, about a million people manage to scratch a living out of the Atacama, inhabiting the few oases and the Pacific fringes of the desert where coastal mists supply just enough moisture to sustain algae, mosses and the odd cactus.

The terrain is 15 million years old and there is a wealth of remains from a Paleo-Indian civilization. Incan artefacts and mummies have been found perfectly preserved, desiccated in the sterile desert soil. The desert is the world's largest source of saltpetre, and 40 per cent of the world's lithium reserves are to be found in Salar de Atacama, a 3,000 sq km (1,160 sq mi) salt lake covered with a bizarre white crust. The desert landscape is visually superb – a weird lunar scenery straight out of Salvador Dali, where the amazing shapes and extraordinary tones of the earth contrast with reflections from the sky in the salt lagoons. The main oasis is the village of San Pedro, from where there are views of the vast peaks of the Andes to the east, and the Salt Mountains, moulded by erosion into giant mineral sculptures, to the west.

Isla Grande de Tierra del Fuego

WHEN TO GO:
November to March
HOW TO GET THERE:
By air, from Buenos Aires or Santiago to Ushuaia (Argentina), or from Punta Arenas to Porvenir (Chile); by bus, via Rio Gallegos to Ushuaia.
HIGHLIGHTS:
Parakeets, condors, kingfishers, owls, firecrown hummingbirds and hosts of waterfowl.
World class trout fishing in the rivers near Rio Grande, the ranching centre.
The Tierra del Fuego National Park near Ushuaia, including the archeological sites of 'los concheros' and the extraordinary coastline of Lapataia Bay.
The seals, sea lions and penguin rookeries along the Beagle Channel.
The enormous (380 cells plus vast workshops) 'prison at the end of the world', the original raison d'etre of Ushuaia.
The Museo Tierra del Fuego in Porvenir, Chile – which tells the story of the gold rush.

The Island of Fire got its name from Magellan in 1520, inspired by the open fires that the local Yamana Indians carried in their fishing boats and in their camps to keep warm. The climate is worse than inhospitable. It snows in summer, and it's very windy, foggy, and wet as well as bitterly cold. Inland, some

An Argentine prairie

areas actually have a polar climate. All the rules say no trees should grow here, but Tierra del Fuego's sub-Antarctic forests are unique in the world, and tree cover (albeit so twisted and stunted by the wind that they are called 'flag trees') extends almost to the tip of South America.

Tierra del Fuego is defined by the Straits of Magellan and the Beagle Channel, both of which link the Atlantic and Pacific Oceans. It's divided politically between Chile and Argentina, who both jealously

YOU SHOULD KNOW:
Tierra del Fuego lights up popular imagination as 'the world's most southerly point'. It isn't. That honour belongs to Islote Aguila ('Aguila Islet'), the southernmost of the Diego Ramirez islands, and therefore of South America, about 100 km (60 mi) southwest of Cape Horn in the Drake Passage.

The small town of Ushuaia hugs the shore.

guard their rights to oil, gas and minerals. Both countries, however, have been quick to see the rising value of eco-tourism, and to appreciate the enhanced value of co-operation. On both sides, the rather shameful history of colonial depredations wreaked on the indigenous Yamana and Selk'nam by gold prospectors, whalers, and commercial hunters are now a matter of shared 'heritage' – and both in Ushuaia, by far the biggest city on the island, and Argentina's hub for most visitors, and Porvenir, Chile's main town far to the north, the museums of ethnic culture are a revelation. The ancient tribal creation mythologies add the dimension of human warmth to one of the world's most forbidding landscapes.

Tierra del Fuego is great for big sea-run brown trout and oceanic marine mammals with birds to match. You get lakes and glaciers, mountains, prairies, swamps and dense forests with the magnified beauty of wilderness on a continental scale. It is a harsh, disturbing place – and intensely rewarding to visit.

Explore the Península Valdés

If you are in search of an escape from the mundane, you would be hard put to find anywhere more inspiring than the windswept shores and blue waters of the Patagonian coast. This magical region of multi-coloured pebble beaches, steep cliffs, jagged rocks, and miles of sand flats is one of the most precious wildlife habitats in the world where, amongst a plethora of sea and land creatures, you can see dolphins playing, orcas out on a seal hunt, and the largest southern right whale breeding grounds in the world.

The drive from Puerto Madryn, on Golfo Nuevo, along the Ameghino Isthmus to the tip of the World Heritage wilderness of Península Valdés, plunges you

HOW:
By car
WHEN TO GO:
June to December to see southern right whales and orcas. Wildlife is at its peak October-November.
TIME IT TAKES:
Although this is only a 200-km (125-mi) drive, the roads are mainly unpaved. You should allow 2-3 days if you want to explore the peninsula properly.

Orca whales hunting sea lion pups.

HIGHLIGHTS:
Watch southern right
whales from El Doradillo
Beach.
Boat ride out to sea from
Puerto Piràmides to see
dolphins and whales.
The sea lion and seal
colonies.
Diving from Punta Pardelas
beach.

straight into the savage beauty of the natural world.
You can hear the southern right whales calling to each
other as you watch them play in the water along the
remote shores of El Doradillo beach. You drive along
dirt tracks through desolate country of steppe and
saltpans where guanacos, rheas, maras and grey foxes
roam at will among the sheep. On the mudflats of
Puento Norte, while you watch the elephant seals and
sea lions, you will see opportunistic orcas lurking
offshore ready to pounce on any unprotected pup and

drag it into the water. At Valdés Caleta, a long gravel spit, you can observe a colony of Magellan penguins among the thousands of seabirds that congregate here.

At the end of the road, at Punta Delgada lighthouse on the southeastern tip of the peninsula, as you gaze down from the high cliffs at the huge colony of elephant seals on the beach below and out over the endless spread of the Atlantic Ocean, you feel you have reached the very edge of the earth, far beyond the clutches of the man-made world.

YOU SHOULD KNOW:
Península Valdés is a protected nature reserve and you must pay a fee to enter.
You can also see the largest Magellan penguin colony in the world at Punto Tombo, 110 km (70 mi) south of Puerto Madryn.

A group of Magellan penguins

Lau Islands

WHEN TO GO:
Unless you like singing in the rain, make it the cooler, drier months from April to October.

HOW TO GET THERE:
Stand by for a true flashback in modern tourist terms – the only way is to catch one of the cargo boats that sporadically serve the Lau Islands from Suva, then island-hop by fishing boat.

HIGHLIGHTS:
Wonderful wood-carvings and striking masi painting (on cloth made from the paper of the mulberry tree) produced by the locals.
Some of Fiji's most pristine dive sites – best to bring your own boat (and live on it).
The caves – Qara Bulu on Lakeba (once a prison) and the large sea cave on Vanua Balavu (used by people over a thousand years ago).

YOU SHOULD KNOW:
Anyone for cricket? Unlike the rest of Fiji (rugby mad, soccer crazy), the Lau islanders prefer cricket, and supply almost all the national team's players.

To discover the true South Pacific of yesteryear it is necessary to mount an expedition to the Lau Islands. This cluster of one hundred or more islands and islets makes up Fiji's remote Eastern Archipelago.

Around 30 are inhabited – by villagers who remain entirely traditional. To the south are low coral isles and to the north high volcanic islands, making for a wonderful variety of scenery. They are notable for producing a disproportionate number of people who have become prominent in the country's business and political life, including prime ministers and a president. This is the place where Melanesian Fiji comes closest to Polynesian Tonga, acting as a mixing point for the two cultures. Tongan influence is apparent in names, language, food and buildings – Lauan houses tend to be rounded in Tongan fashion rather than square in Fijian style. The island of Lakeba in the south is a traditional meeting place, and one of the few islands where the intrepid traveller will find guest-houses.

Another is Kaimbu, a private resort island. Accommodation may also be found on Vanua Balavu, the archipelago's second-largest island and biggest in the northern group. It has an extensive reef system, steep undercut cliffs, hot springs and the Yanuyanu Island Resort built to advance tourist development in this hitherto 'undiscovered' archipelago (though a permit to visit must be obtained from the Ministry of Foreign Affairs in Suvu!). There is also an airfield and a small copra port on the island.

For those of adventurous bent who don't rely on advanced booking, the Lau Islands can deliver the trip of a lifetime. Catch it while you can – it's only a matter of time before the modern world arrives.

An aerial view of the northern Lau group

Kangaroo Island

WHEN TO GO:
June through to August is fabulous. The countryside is lush and the wildlife active during the day: kangaroos are popping out of the pouch, koalas, Southern right whales are steaming by on migration, and the male echidnas are out looking for mates. September to November sees Kangaroo Island in full bloom, and eucalyptus oil in full production.

Cape du Couedic lighthouse

Kangaroo in both name and nature, this large island just 13 km (8 mi) off the South Australian mainland has remained relatively untouched for thousands of years; and as such is an unblemished microcosm of the vast red continent. Towering cliffs protect the northern shores, giving way to more exposed sandy beaches in the south. Bushwalking is pretty compulsory, and trails meander across the national and conservation parks that cover a third of the island.

Wild koalas hug the trees and kangaroos hop down the streets. Isolated from the ravages of European diseases and introduced species that afflicted their near neighbours, the native animals and plants have flourished – echidnas, platypuses, possums and penguins can all be ticked off the wildlife fanatic's list.

In 1800, Captain Matthew Flinders was commissioned by the British Government to chart the southern coastline of Terra Australis in HMS *Investigator*. He first sighted this island in March 1802, came ashore and named it Kangaroo Island, after dining well on wild kangaroo meat. Just weeks later he spotted a French ship on the horizon, under the command of Nicholas Baudin. Despite their two countries being at war, the two men were civil,

A koala clings to the branch of a tree.

HOW TO GET THERE:
By regular ferries (45 mins) from Cape Jervis to Penneshaw. By air – from Adelaide (30 mins)

HIGHLIGHTS:
Flinders Chase National Park – incredible rock formations including Remarkable Rocks and Admiral's Arch.
Little penguins on parade around Kingscote and Penneshaw – as they head back from the water to their seaside burrows for the night.
Surfing or swimming at Vivonne Bay – Australia's top beach for clear, clean waters and privacy.
Emu Ridge Eucalyptus Distillery is the only commercial distillery of its type in South Australia, still employing 600 islanders.

YOU SHOULD KNOW:
Here you can taste honey from the only known pure strain of Ligurian bee in the world. Twelve hives were imported from Liguria, Italy in the 1880s and in splendid island isolation they have remained pure – untouched by other breeds of bees, and producing true nectar of the gods.

exchanging ideas and even vital supplies.

Baudin went on to map the south and west coastlines, leaving many French names in his wake: Ravine des Casoars, D'Estress Bay and Cape de Couedic – now home to a colony of New Zealand fur seals.

Experienced divers may discover one of the 50 or so wrecks that litter this rocky coastline. Following

the earliest recorded shipwreck in 1847, the first
lighthouse in South Australia was built at Cape
Willoughby, and stands to this day – 27 metres (89 ft)
high and a healthy climb to the top. Ferries landing at
Penneshaw on the eastern tip make it a hotspot for
tourists, but it is easy enough to get away into the
wilds and delight in this well-preserved refuge.

*Amazing rock
formations in Flinders
Chase National Park*

Norfolk Island

A tiny jewel set in the azure seas of the South Pacific, Norfolk Island is just 8 km (5 mi) long, and 1,600 km (994 mi) northeast of Sydney. It is the biggest of a cluster of three islands on the Norfolk Ridge, fringed by coral reefs and crowned by pristine rainforest and some of the world's tallest tree ferns.

On 10 October 1774, James Cook first landed on this diminutive island and named it in honour of the

RIGHT: Anson Bay

The old penal settlement at Kingston

WHEN TO GO:
Idyllic in December-January,
with temperatures ranging
from 12ºC (54º F) at night
to 19-21ºC (66-70º F) in
the day.
HOW TO GET THERE:
Regular flights from Sydney,
Brisbane, Newcastle and
Auckland
HIGHLIGHTS:
Bounty Day – 8 June. When
the islanders re-enact the
landing of their ancestors on
the island.
Kingston – built by convicts
of the second penal colony,
with many historic buildings.
Bushwalks through the
National Park – to see some
of the 40 plants unique to
the island.
Lazing under the Norfolk
Island Pines – up to 57 m
(187 ft) tall.
A hot-stone massage with
heated basalt stones from
the nearby beach.
YOU SHOULD KNOW:
English is the main language
here, but the islanders still
speak to each other in
'Norfolk' – a mix of 18th
century English and
Polynesian. *Wataweih
yorlye*? means 'How are
you?'

then Duchess of Norfolk. Convicts started to arrive fourteen years later and over time it gained quite a reputation, becoming known as 'hell in the Pacific'. Then in 1856, descendants of the Bounty mutineers with their Tahitian wives and children sailed for five weeks from Pitcairn Island to settle on Norfolk Island. These new settlers brought with them a distinct culture and language, and many held mutineers' names such as Adams, Buffett, Christian and McCoy. From that day, Norfolk Island began its steady climb out of hell and into heaven.

Once sustained by agriculture and fishing, visitors now keep the island alive. But traditional culture remains deep-rooted – with dancing, singing and a unique cuisine. Banana dumplings, fried fish and Hihi pie, concocted with periwinkles, can be sampled at one of the fine restaurants scattered across the island.

The blue waters around Norfolk Island are teeming with fish, and there are countless fishing charters and scuba-diving trips out to the reef to explore this kaleidoscope underwater world. In the sheltered waters of Emily Bay, you can also indulge in some lazy swimming and snorkelling, and endless relaxation.

Norfolk Island is favoured by well-heeled Australians and New Zealanders, and a few millionaires have migrated to this tax-free haven. There are over seventy low-tax shops and many eager customers. Yet the island seems to balance the old and the new perfectly – honouring its Pitcairn people, its rich environment and its visitors.

Cradle Mountain-Lake St Clare National Park

Part of Tasmania's Wilderness Area World Heritage Site, the Cradle Mountain-Lake St Clare National Park is a stunning area of craggy ridges and crests, valleys scooped out by glaciers, cirques and lakes, dropping down through alpine heathland, button grass, wildflower meadows, pine and beech woods to areas of ancient rainforest.

The hike up the 1,545-m (5,068-ft.) Cradle Mountain and back takes about eight hours, but there are easier walks on its lower slopes and the three-hour walk

WHAT IS IT:
A beautiful glacial landscape in Tasmania
HOW TO GET THERE:
By road from Launceston
WHEN TO GO:
Spring to autumn
NEAREST TOWN:
Sheffield 50km (30 mi)

The Ducane hut, one of nine public huts along the route

The peaks of Cradle Mountain as seen from Dove Lake

PREVIOUS: Hikers on Cradle Mountain

around the beautiful Dove Lake is not to be missed. Cradle Mountain is in the north of the park, and Lake St Clare – Australia's deepest freshwater lake – in the far south. The six-day hike from one to the other – known as the Overland Track – is one of the most popular in Australia, and draws walkers from all over the world. It leads through some of the wildest pristine landscapes on the island, with glacial lakes, icy streams and waterfalls and spectacular views of

the mountains above. There are nine huts spaced along the 80-km (50-mi) trail, in which walkers can make overnight stops – even in summer it can be very cold at night and snow is not unheard of in the higher areas.

Other activities on offer in the park include rafting on the Franklin River, an exhilarating ride that takes you through even more beautiful areas of pristine wilderness.

Lake Manapouri

WHAT IS IT:
The deepest of South Island's southern glacial lakes

HOW TO GET THERE:
By road from Invercargill. It's also possible to take a cruise across the lake from Pearl Harbour which is located on the south eastern corner of the lake.

WHEN TO GO:
Late spring to early autumn

NEAREST TOWN:
Manapouri

The deepest of South Island's southern glacial lakes, Lake Manapouri is a quite haven. Surrounded on three sides by high mountains, which remain snow-capped for a large part of the year, this beautiful lake and its surroundings are popular with wilderness lovers from all over the country.

There are several walking and hiking trails that pass by, or close to, the lake, of which the 67-km (42-mi) Kepler Track and the Circle Track are the best known. These lead through native bush and require a degree of fitness. There is also a longer-distance track to Dusky Sound in the south-west. In winter and spring, the higher parts of the routes will be closed because of snow. The lake saw the beginning of the early Green movement in New Zealand when in the early 1960s conservationists fought, and won against, the proposal to raise

the water levels 30 m (100 ft) to enlarge the reservoir for the Manapouri Power Station, which would have drowned most of the thirty-three islands dotted within the lake. The power station was built, but the water levels are maintained as close to natural fluctuation levels as possible. The bays, islands and beaches are beautiful and there is a rich array of local plants and birds, including the endearing tui, which can often be seen by the lakeshore.

The sun sets over the lake.

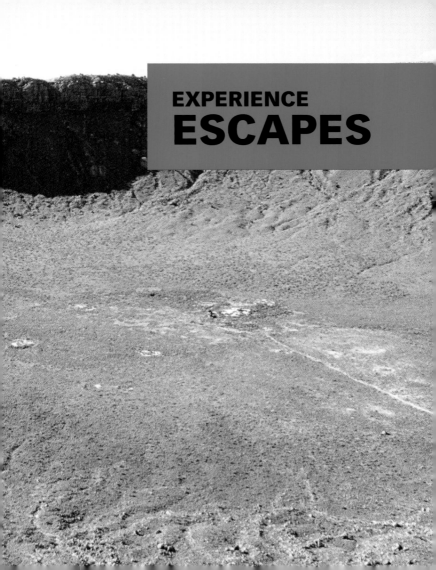

EXPERIENCE
ESCAPES

Westman Islands Festival

WHEN:
The first weekend of August
WHERE:
Heimaey
BEST FOR:
Music and partying
YOU SHOULD KNOW:
This is now the biggest festival in Iceland. It began in 1874 when celebrations for the 1,000-year anniversary of the settlement of Iceland were organized on the mainland and the Westman islanders were unable to travel because of bad weather conditions. They decided to stage their own celebration, and have continued doing so ever since. Ironically, thousands of mainlanders now make their way to Heimaey each year.

Heimaey is the largest of the remote Westman Islands that lie off Iceland's southern coast. With a population of just over 4,000, it is also the only one that is inhabited. The Westmans are part of a young, active, underwater volcanic system and in 1973 there was a dramatic eruption on Heimaey when a new cone, Eldfell, appeared where once had lain a meadow. Lava flowed, buildings were buried or burned by red-hot ash, and the whole world focused its attention on Iceland.

Heimaey is also famous for its festival. Held each summer, when the days are 21 hours long, thousands of people travel from the mainland and wider Europe to party 24/7 for three days on this beautiful island. There are hotels, but most choose to camp at the centre of the action – the locals in large, white tents. This is a music festival, but it is also a 'drinkathon' and a love-in – many couples happily make out in the most surreal of locations: a natural, grassy amphitheatre in the hollow of a volcano.

There are three highlights during the weekend. At midnight on Friday a gigantic bonfire is lit, warming those who have not yet consumed sufficient vodka to feel no pain at all. The drinking of vodka is utterly stupendous, enabling people to roll en masse down the hill without breaking any bones, and timid foreigners to test out the local delicacy – smoked puffin.

Saturday night's treat is a fantastic firework display, and the Sunday night special features a glorious singsong for the audience, who join Heimaey's beloved Arni Johnsen in renditions of traditional folksongs. At midnight the site glows with a ring of red torches, symbolizing the volcanic eruption. The audience go wild, dancing and drinking the night away for the third night running.

PREVIOUS: The viewing platform over the Arizona Meteor Crater

Fireworks illuminate the locals' white tents.

Notting Hill Carnival

If you think the world's biggest street carnival is in Rio, you're right. But – perhaps surprisingly – second prize goes to London, with the Notting Hill Carnival attracting up to two million people each year. It has grown from an indoor community event aimed at improving race relations after the Notting Hill Riots of 1958, moving outside in 1964 as a gathering for local folk. But it soon acquired the Caribbean character that has become a hallmark – plus a large and ever-expanding annual audience.

After trouble when youths and police did battle in the late 1970s, leading to calls (happily resisted) for the event to be banned, it has gone from strength to strength as a peaceful but dynamic celebration of Britain's multicultural society, though the emphasis remains firmly Afro-Caribbean.

The narrow streets of Notting Hill are the carnival's focal point, though recent years have seen the introduction of a 'savannah' area in Hyde Park where related events occur. Children's Day on Sunday sees a shorter parade tailored to families and kids, complete with appropriate entertainments mounted by under-21s supported by floats, elaborate costumes . . . with painted faces all round.

On Monday, the colourful main parade of decorated floats and flamboyant dancers follows a 6.5-km (3-mi) route along the Great West Road, Chepstow Road, Westbourne Grove and Ladbroke Grove. Officially, the carnival consists of four disciplines – costume masquerade, steel band, calypso and SOCA (the fusion Sounds of the Caribbean and Africa). So the all-pervasive feature is the sound of (loud) music, with static sound systems competing lustily with mobile brethren and bands on passing floats. 'Official' music gets keen competition from just about every other style under the sun, resulting in joyful cacophony. The supercharged result is the most vibrant of events – once experienced, never forgotten!

WHEN:
Late August (on a Sunday and the following Bank Holiday Monday)
WHERE:
Notting Hill, West London
BEST FOR:
Uninhibited calypso capers
YOU SHOULD KNOW:
The National Competition of Steel – a keenly fought contest between traditional Caribbean steel bands – takes place in Hyde Park on the previous Saturday.

LEFT and NEXT:
Colourful costumes at
the Notting Hill
Carnival

La Tomatina

WHEN:
Late August
WHERE:
Buñol, Valencia
BEST FOR:
Watching rather than
participating
YOU SHOULD KNOW:
It's necessary to get up
early in order to secure a
place in the central square
where the tomato fight
takes place – La Tomatina is
now so well known and
popular that latecomers get
marooned a few streets
away from the serious
action.
There is limited
accommodation in Buñol so
most people who wish to
enjoy La Tomatina stay in
nearby Valencia – 38 km (24
mi) away – and travel in by
bus or train.

This is not an event likely to be enjoyed by those who wince at the price of fresh tomatoes in the supermarket, for La Tomatina sees literally millions of the plump red fruits wantonly destroyed. But what entertainment! Whilst the 'Battle of the Tomatoes' rages on the last Wednesday of August the

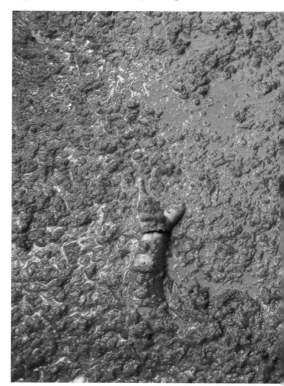

celebrations start a few days before, creating a wonderful festive atmosphere in the small Valencian town of Buñol.

Indeed, La Tomatina has become one of Spain's most famous fiestas, with thousands of people arriving to join the general brouhaha that lasts for a week before the tomatoes fly. It's all in honour of the town's patron saints, St Louis Bertrand and the Mother of the

A reveller covered in tomato pulp

An overhead view shows vivid colour – and lots of bodies!

God of the Defenceless (aka the Virgin Mary). If that sounds a little serious, the style in which these worthies are saluted is anything but. There are street parades, music, dancing and fireworks. On the night before the big fight a serious paella-cooking contest takes place, with the tasty results much appreciated by hungry festival goers.

The next morning, shop fronts are covered in plastic sheeting and lorries loaded with over-ripe tomatoes arrive in the town square, Plaza del Pueblo. As brave souls try in turn to climb a greasy pole and claim the prize ham that waits on top, a water cannon fires and the mayhem begins. Health and safety regulations demand that combatants should wear goggles and gloves, and that tomatoes must be squished before being used as missiles. These are ignored, along with the injunction that no clothing may be ripped, and it's a case of every man (or woman) for himself (or herself). After an hour the water cannon fires again and La Tomatina is over for another year as the fire trucks move in for the big hosedown. Mouth-watering!

The Blue Grotto

The southern Italian isle of Capri, beloved of the emperors Augustus and Tiberius, lies off the Sorrentine Peninsula at the south of the Bay of Naples. It is predominantly made of limestone and this soft rock has allowed the sea to carve numerous sea caves into its cliffs. The most famous of these is the Blue Grotto, on the south coast, which the emperors supposedly used as a private bath. Once under the low entrance to the cave, visitors are surrounded by blue light that fades as the cave recedes away into the darkness. But where does the eerie blue light come from? It is, in fact, sunlight getting into the cave though another, submerged, entrance and being reflected off the white limestone and sand on the cave's floor, so lighting the water from underneath. If the entrance to the cave were higher, sunlight would get in that way, too, and drown out the magical blue glow.

Depending on the height of the waves, guides on the boat trips, that are the only way to get into the cave, may ask visitors to lie down to avoid bumping their heads. If you shut your eyes on the way through the entrance, the effect of the blue around you as you open them is even more startling.

WHAT IS IT:
A remarkable accident of nature
HOW TO GET THERE:
By boat from Naples or Sorrento to Capri's Marina Grande, then a local boat trip
WHEN TO GO:
Summer
NEAREST TOWN:
Capri town 3 km (2 mi)
YOU SHOULD KNOW:
The guides sometimes sing in the caves.

NEXT: The eerie blue light silhouettes boaters in the grotto.

221

Holi

WHEN:
Usually March (at the full moon of the Hindu month Purnima)
WHERE:
Jaipur and all over northern India
BEST FOR:
Elephants and colours
YOU SHOULD KNOW:
Huge quantities of pink powder fly around Jaipur on Holi Day. Pink is, for Indians, the colour of hospitality. Maharaja Ram Singh had the whole city of Jaipur painted for the Prince of Wales' visit in 1876 and the colour scheme of this big, chaotic and fascinating city remains unchanged.

Holi, also called the Festival of Colours, is a celebration of the end of winter and one of northern India's most exuberant festivals. Although this is a Hindu festival, people of all faiths participate. On the eve of Holi (Purnima Day) bonfires are lit in the streets to destroy the evil demon Holika and on Holi Day itself everyone throws coloured powders and water at each other.

In Jaipur, the annual Elephant Festival is held on Purnima Day. A fabulous procession of elephants, dressed in fringed silks and brocades, tusks wound with beads and garlands, toenails painted and ankles circled by jingling bracelets, skins painted with geometric patterns and psychedelic flowers, heads proudly out to the sports ground. After a grand parade, huge crowds watch Rajasthani musicians and

dancers in fabulous costumes, an elephant beauty contest and elephant polo matches and races. After firework displays, everyone heads back to the city. Bales of hay are burnt in the streets to consume the ills of winter, and partying continues late into the night.

With its dusky pink streets and rosy palaces, the old city is always colourful; on Holi Day it becomes dazzlingly polychromatic. For visitors venturing out, old clothes are essential – though some groups of revellers ask permission to dab colours on face, hair and hands, most throw blizzards of powder and fountains of coloured water at tourists and friends, men and women, old and young – even at bank managers!

'Bombs' – balloons filled with water and powder and dropped from roofs – explode all around. The Festival of Colours is joyful, good-natured and very, very messy.

An Indian elephant is painted for the festival.

LEFT: An explosion of colours

NEXT: Children play with coloured powder.

Tokyo May Basho

Exclusively Japanese, steeped in history, tradition and Shinto ritual, sumo wrestling is the most exciting contact sport in the world. It is blindingly quick. Two super-heavyweights face each other across a 4.5-m (15-ft) diameter clay *dohyo* (ring). After a lengthy exchange of stamping, stretching and tossing salt – purification rites shared by a referee holding a fan as an emblem of authority, and whose every action is

prescribed by Japan's most ancient history – they hurl themselves at each other in a blur of action.

There are about 80 recognized ways of forcing an opponent out of the *dohyo* (if any part of the body other than the soles of your feet touch the ground, you lose), and top sumo wrestlers can attempt several in the few seconds that most bouts last. Their speed, skill and aggression make it look like whole-body fencing.

There are just six, two-week-long *Hon-basho* (tournaments determining ranking) in the sumo calendar, and Natsu Basho, held in Tokyo in May, is one of the most splendid. The best *rikishi* (wrestlers) in the sumo world meet in the 11,000-seat Kokugikan.

You'll see the action up close if you get there early at 09.00, but the top ranks don't fight until 16.00, when the best seats are taken by aficionados in traditional Japanese dress. The constant ceremony and ritual creates an atmosphere of timeless history by the time the top ranks of all – *yokozuna* (grand champion) and *ozeki* (champion) – step forward. Each is already a national hero, and known by a special sumo nickname. Their fights are the stuff of legend and scandal. In 2008, when the first foreigner (the Bulgarian *ozeki*, known as Kotooshu) won the Emperor's Cup at the Natsu Basho, the national shame was overshadowed by the failure of the defeated *yokozuna*, Asashoryu, to behave with the decorum demanded of his exalted rank.

WHEN:
Two weeks in mid May
WHERE:
Ryogoku Kokugikan
(sumo wrestling hall), Tokyo
BEST FOR:
Sport, history, religion and culture
YOU SHOULD KNOW:
When the *rikishi* clap violently before a bout, they are demonstrating they are unarmed. By contrast, the referee in his splendid traditional dress carries a small dagger. It symbolizes his willingness to commit ritual suicide if his impartiality is called into question. Honour is everything in sumo.

LEFT: Two sumo wrestlers engage in battle.

NEXT: The sumo wrestlers' ceremonial entrance

229

Lake of Stars Music Festival

WHEN:
October
WHERE:
Senga Bay on Lake Malawi
BEST FOR:
Chilled atmosphere and
beautiful lakeside setting
YOU SHOULD KNOW:
The campsite at the festival
is surprisingly well
organized with excellent
sanitary facilities. While the
waters of Lake Malawi look
very inviting, you should
probably resist the
temptation to swim here
due to the presence of the
bilharzia parasite. Though
it's easily cured once
diagnosed, bilharzia has
serious consequences if left
untreated.

Lake of Stars is the brainchild of a British DJ who lost his heart to Malawi during his gap year travels. Moved by the material poverty of this breathtakingly beautiful country, he set about promoting Malawi's music at the same time as raising money for UNICEF. A festival seemed a good idea, so he organized one – just like that. Even though Lake of Stars has only been going since 2004, it has already achieved renown as an ultra-cool event, quite unlike anything else in the world.

The three-day festival is held at Senga Bay on the western shore of Lake Malawi, a beautiful stretch of coast with miles of immaculate white sandy beaches. The audience is an unlikely mix of trendsetters, globetrotters, expatriate workers and students, joined, as the weekend progresses, by more and more of the local youth, seduced by the revelry. The crowd grows to about 1,500, gathered around a couple of bamboo stages, small enough to give a joyful sense of camaraderie so that by the end of the festival the motley horde appears to have transmuted into a strange sort of multi-ethnic tribe, bonded through their shared experience.

Apart from an amazing range of performers, from African jazz players to English DJs, the unique magic of Lake of Stars lies in its incredible ambience and exquisite natural setting: the constantly changing mood of the lake; the energizing beat of the music in the enervating heat of the African sun; the shaded palm-fringed shore and the soft deep sand. At nightfall, people gather round campfires on the beach, jamming and dancing until dawn when the fishermen return with their catch. It doesn't get any more chilled than this.

*Oliver Mtukudzi
performs at the
music festival.*

Icefields Parkway

HOW:
By car
DEPART:
Lake Louise, AB
WHEN TO GO:
May to September offers
the best weather.
TIME IT TAKES:
Around four hours without
stopping, but allow a full
day for picnic breaks.
HIGHLIGHTS:
The Columbia Icefield – a
chance to witness a pristine
wilderness.
Lake Louise – with its
turquoise lake and
overhanging glacier.
The Crossings – a chance to
reflect and anticipate.
Arriving in Jasper, a rather
special town set on a small
plateau surrounded by a
spectacular panoramic
mountain backdrop.
YOU SHOULD KNOW:
Even in good weather the
sheer elevation of this
highway can mean that road
conditions can change
rapidly, so come prepared
for all eventualities.

The magnificence of the Icefields Parkway (Hwy 93) can scarcely be overstated – a 230 km (144 mi) road from Lake Louise to Jasper through the heart of the Rockies, it ranks as one of the world's ultimate drives. Its seemingly unending succession of enormous peaks, vast glaciers, iridescent lakes, wild-flower meadows, wildlife and forests – capped by the sheer majesty of the Columbia Icefield – is utterly overwhelming.

Fur traders and First Nations peoples dubbed it the Wonder Trail, though the current road owes much to the depression era works programme and it was only opened in 1940 in its present incarnation.

Leaving the iconic image of Lake Louise behind you, the first 40 km (25 mi) of the road climbs steadily north through forest, until you reach the alpine meadow at Bow Summit, the journey's highest point. The next section, which drops down to the Saskatchewan River, offers the best chance to see black bears and moose. The Crossings marks the transition from the jaw-droppingly good to the truly awesome. This 50 km (31 mi) section is famous the world over for its breathtaking scenery as Mount Athabasca and the Columbia Glacier heave into view.

View of the Rockies from the Parkway

Mountain goats, bighorn sheep and elk are common along the final 100 km (62 mi) of the Parkway. The road ascends Tangle Ridge, then drops down through forest and follows the Sunwapta and Athabasca rivers into the charming little town of Jasper. The outstanding features of this final leg are the Sunwapta and Athabasca Falls and the opportunity to spot grizzly bears and mountain caribou.

Although over a million people make the trip each year to experience this 'window on the wilderness', the sheer vastness of the landscape still means it can rarely seem crowded.

Maine Lobster Festival

WHEN:
Late July/early August
WHERE:
Harbor Park, Rockland,
Maine
BEST FOR:
Gastronomy (at low, low
prices) and New England
local traditions
YOU SHOULD KNOW:
The local obsession is
summarized by the sole
neon sign displayed in the
community of Ogonquit.
It reads: 'Rooms. Cable.
Air-con. Lobster.'

*A young boy competing
in the Great Crate Race.*

If ever a determinedly local festival deserved an
international reputation it's the Maine Lobster
Festival. For five days in late July or early August, the
little fishing port of Rockland – sheltered by a granite
headland among the hundreds of rugged fjords of
Maine's northern coast – dresses up to welcome a
total of more than 100,000 guests to a programme of
parades, contests and games designed to entertain
them in between gorging on several tons of the finest
soft-shell lobster in the world. Lobsters are so
plentiful in the area that the festival began in 1947 as
a way for fishermen to dispose of their catch. Too
fragile to be shipped to Boston or New York, the
lobsters cost $1 for all you could eat. These days, $20
will get you three whole
lobsters (with a plastic bib
and some chips)!

This isn't the Maine of
gentle, sandy coves,
hauteur and huge
Kennebunkport mansions.
Rockland's grandeur is the
honesty of its democratic,
blue-collar inclusivity. The
lobsters are cooked in the
world's biggest lobster
broiler – capable of
holding 545 kg (1,200 lb)
at a time – endearingly
disguised as a 'lighthouse'
and eaten on a series of
long benches inside a
marquee, which can feel
like a Turkish bath. It's so
extraordinary to be eating
one of the great delicacies

One of Maine's finest!

of the world by the shovelful, tearing exquisite morsels with your bare hands in circumstances more like a very cheerful canteen than fine dining. That's when you realize that there are just as many locals as visitors present – and it's their strength of identity that makes being at the Lobster Festival feel like a privilege.

Between lobsters, parades, bands and more lobsters, check out the Lobster Crate Racing: you have to 'walk on water' by running across 50 bobbing lobster crates tethered across a neck of the harbour. Most people get a chilly Atlantic ducking after ten crates; the record, back and forth without stopping, is over 3,000!

Meteor Crater, Arizona

HOW TO GET THERE:
By road
WHEN TO GO:
October to May
NEAREST TOWN:
Winslow 32 km (20 mi)
DON'T MISS:
The charming towns of
Flagstaff and Sedona
YOU SHOULD KNOW:
The crater is still owned and
run by the Barringer family.
An entry fee is payable.
Visitors may not enter the
crater itself.

Meteor Crater is a huge, almost circular hole in the arid Arizona desert. It is 1,200 m (4,100 ft) in diameter and 173 m (570 ft) deep, and has a rim of rocks and boulders rising some 45 m (150 ft) above the surrounding area. Although there are other, larger meteorite craters in the world, the studies made of this one provided the first proof of meteoritic impact upon the earth's surface.

Estimated to be some 50,000 years old, the meteorite, formed of nickel iron, was about 50 m (165 ft) across. It hit the ground at about 12.8 km (8 mi) per second, and roughly half its bulk was vapourized as it ploughed through our atmosphere before impact. Even so, it will have produced an

238

incredible explosion, in the region of 150 times the force of the atomic bombs at Hiroshima and Nagasaki.

Daniel Moreau Barringer, a mining engineer, originally suggested that this was a meteorite crater in 1903. Prior to this it had been thought to be the result of volcanic activity. Barringer's company bought the crater and found that it had been caused by a violent impact. His conclusions were met with disbelief from the scientific community so he decided to prove them by digging up the remains of the meteorite, not knowing that it had disintegrated when it hit. He spent 26 years drilling for metallic iron without success, and in 1929 he died, his hypothesis still unproven. It was not until 1960 that Eugene M. Shoemaker found two forms of silica in the crater that can only be created through an impact event, and was able to conclusively confirm Barringer's theory.

An aerial view of Meteor Crater

239

Las Vegas

WHAT IS IT:
The gambling centre of the United States
WHEN TO GO:
Summers are hot here, but everything is air conditioned, making this a year round centre of entertainment of all kinds.
WHAT IS THERE TO DO:
Gamble, watch live entertainment, eat at gourmet restaurants, play golf, shop, stay in luxurious resorts or just hang out by the pool. Day trips to the Grand Canyon are also possible.
HOLLYWOOD CONNECTION:
The Hangover and both versions of *Ocean's Eleven* were filmed here as well as *CSI Las Vegas*.
ALSO KNOWN AS:
Sin City or the entertainment capital of the world.

Las Vegas is known for many things: glitz, glamour, ostentation, gambling, entertainment, debauchery, shopping and excess. The most populous city in the state of Nevada, it is the largest founded in the twentieth century, and is the centre of gambling in the United States.

Beginning as a stopover en route to the pioneer trails to the west, Las Vegas became a popular railway town in the early twentieth century, serving as a staging point for the mines in the surrounding area, that shipped their goods out to the country from its station. With the growth of the railway, Las Vegas became less important, but the construction of the Hoover Dam injected a new vitality into Las Vegas and the city has never looked back.

The increase in tourism caused by the dam and the legalization of gambling led to the advent of the casino-hotels for which Las Vegas is famous. In the mid- to late-1940s a small building boom included several hotel-casinos by the two-lane main road leading into Las Vegas from Los Angeles, and this is now home to today's 'Strip'. Among the most notable buildings was Bugsy Siegel's Flamingo Hotel, with its neon signs and pink flamingo lawn ornaments that opened in 1946.

In the 1950s, resort building continued to accelerate. Wilbur Clark, once a hotel bellman in San Diego, opened the Desert Inn in 1950. Two years later, Milton Prell opened the Sahara Hotel on the site of the old Club Bingo. The Sands Hotel opened that same year. In 1955, the Riviera Hotel became the first Strip highrise at nine storeys. Other resorts that opened during the building boom begun in the 1950s included the Royal Nevada, Dunes, Tropicana and Stardust hotels. During this time the entertainment industry in Las Vegas took off. In the 1950s Las Vegas became synonymous with the Rat Pack. Entertainment, not just gambling, became the reason to visit the city. For 43 years Frank Sinatra played to sold-out shows in resorts from the Desert Inn to the Sands to the MGM Grand. Sinatra's Rat Pack image of all-night singing, dancing, drinking and womanizing brought a new demographic to the Strip. As the Rat Pack charmed Eisenhower-era America, the Strip continued to expand.

The 1970s saw a decline in Las Vegas tourism. Las Vegas had become a run-down town with little to bring in the crowds. The local government and hoteliers decided it was time to clean up their act. In the late 1980s the Strip was reborn with the construction of the 3,049-room Mirage at a cost of $630 million. Featuring a white tiger habitat, a dolphin pool, an elaborate swimming pool and waterfall and a man-made volcano belching fire, the days of glamour were officially back. Treasure Island, with its full scale pirate ship that engages in combat with a British frigate in its nightly shows, sinking its

The sign says it all!

enemy as a grand finale, is another example of the more recent excesses available here.

The Excalibur, a 4,000 room colossus was the next to open in 1990. The imaginative medieval 'castle' has some floors devoted solely to non-gambling entertainment for children and the young at heart including court jesters who perform in public areas. The showroom features jousting on horseback by knights of King Arthur's court.

The Bellagio and Eiffel Tower lit up at night

As the luxury resorts appeared so did the retailers. Here you can find nearly every brand on earth from Tiffany to Gucci to Prada and Valentino. Entertainment has also made a resurgence with performers such as Cirque de Soleil, Elton John, Barry Manilow and Celine Dion.

Other spectacular hotels and resorts have continued to spring up including the MGM Grand, New York-New York, the Palms, the Venetian and the Bellagio. Inspired by the Lake Como resort of Bellagio in Italy, the Bellagio is famed for its its 3.2 ha (8-acre) artificial lake between the hotel and the Strip. The lake encompasses thousands of fountains, their high streams of water lit by a rainbow of coloured lights, flowing to the accompanying music.

The new CityCenter – a 'city within a city' built on a 27 ha (67 acre) site – opened in 2010 and offers yet more hotels, restaurants, up-market stores and, of course, casinos. Vegas is definitely back!

Cenotes and the underground rivers of the Yucatan

WHAT IS IT:
A unique regional freshwater system

HOW TO GET THERE:
From Merida/Chichén Itzá (west) or Playa del Carmen (east)

WHEN TO GO:
November to May

NEAREST TOWN:
Cancun, Valladolid and Chichén Itzá are good regional bases.

YOU SHOULD KNOW:
Open Water diving qualification is necessary for cavern (cenote) diving. Full cave diving (defined as 'beyond sunlight') requires specialist training.

Behind the beach playgrounds of its Caribbean coast lies Yucatan's most magical secret. The whole peninsula is like a giant Swiss cheese made of limestone. Hollowed out by millennia of tropical rainstorms, the porous rock has allowed an entire river system to evolve in its underground heart. About 560 km (350 mi) of criss-crossing waterways have been mapped between Playa del Carmen and Tulum – just ten per cent of the total.

These underground rivers can be long. One twists and turns for 153 km (96 mi) through halls of stalactites and stalagmites as big as jumbo jets and fissures only wide enough for a single diver. In a straight line, the same river covers just 10 km (6 mi). Gigantic meanders like these are the reason why fresh water is distributed so well across the peninsula; why the jungle is so lush, and why the Mayan empire was able to flourish in the region. Then, as now, the underground rivers were accessible via surface sinkwells, or '*cenotes*'. They look like sunlit pools dotted randomly in the dense green, and many have steep walls as if a hole had been punched through the limestone. The Mayans believed the *cenotes* to be gateways to 'the Other

World', and in one way they were right: each *cenote* connects to the only source of fresh water to be found.

Descending into a *cenote* can be like being suspended inside a jewel. Emerald shafts from the holes in the cavern roof cut through the crystal water, itself a shimmer of rainbow fish darting between tree roots and languid trailing foliage. Slightly deeper, where the freshwater meets the seawater at the halocline, the water seems oily and colours divide into a swirling kaleidoscope. Visibility clears as you emerge into full seawater, but the eerie beauty is intensified by the faint green glow now far above. Real magic.

Snorkellers at the entrance to a cave

Cuba

WHEN TO GO:
December to March is the prime beach season but it's brilliant all year round.
HOW TO GET THERE:
By air to Havana, from everywhere except the United States. The US also prevents all passenger ships, and most cruise ships, from calling. US visitors generally come by air, via Cancun, Nassau or Toronto.
HIGHLIGHTS:
Santiago, Cuba's second city, more Caribbean than Havana, with a Creole influence in the palaces, mansions and museums that make it Cuba's historic heart.
The 1795 Tower of the Manaca Iznaga Estate, the manor of a wealthy slaver, and one of the 'ingenios' (19th century sugar mills) set among the Royal palms, waving cane and rolling hills of the Valle de los Ingenios.
The 235 pictographs at Cueva de Punta del Este – called 'the Sistine Chapel of Caribbean Indian art', created circa 800 AD, and the most important of their kind.

NEXT: The view of Havana in the distance from Ernest Hemingway's house, Finca Vigía.

A gloriously retro car cruises a Havana street.

Cuba's history is as shocking as it is lurid. After four centuries of genocide, slavery and savage exploitation, in 1898 Spain lost control of the biggest island in the Caribbean and world's largest sugar producer to its covetous neighbour, the United States. Prevented by its own laws from annexing Cuba (as it had the Philippines, Guam and Puerto Rico), the US instead institutionalized racism, economic slavery, and tourism based on drinking, gambling and prostitution.

When Castro's popular revolution stopped them, the US retaliated by wrecking Cuba's economy, with travel and trade restrictions. However, the lack of fundamental modernization and development on the island has proven to have been a blessing in disguise.

Havana, especially Old Havana, has been restored, not rebuilt as a high-rise mall – and it throbs to the happy syncopations of rumba, sound-splashed on bright colours. Havana is loaded with easy-going character that belies the true vigour and energy driving Cuban culture. More visitors are discovering the real thrill of vibrant beach-life, fabulous nightclubs, ecstatic rhythms, dance and laughter; plus an astounding repository of natural wealth, with all mod cons, but without the paraphernalia of dedicated consumerism that has spoiled so much of the Caribbean.

Twenty-two per cent of Cuba has recently been dedicated to protected reserves, including a 70,000 strong flamingo colony in the Río Máximo-Cagüey wetlands, winding '*mogote*' caves, and the 3,000 rare Cuban crocodiles in the Zapata swamps. These, and the wrought-iron grills, dilapidated mansions, heavenly cigars and mojitos are the things others have built over or excised. Not Cuba. It's got the best of the past, and the future. Go now.

Festival of St Thomas

Guatemala has festivals and parades galore but the daddy of them all takes place at a small white-walled town with strong Mayan roots that perches precipitously in mountains above mysterious mist-filled valleys.

Chichi experiences an extraordinary transformation in the run-up to Christmas, when tens of thousands of people arrive from every corner of Guatemala to join seven days of uninhibited festivities as the Fiesta de Santo Tomás celebrates both the upcoming saint's day of the town's patron on December 21 and also the imminent arrival of Olentzero, a mythical Christmas messenger.

This oh-so-traditional town is always full of vibrant life and elaborate local ritual, centred on the bustling market and historic Church of St Thomas (dating from 1540). But Chichi goes into overdrive for the fiesta – the whole place is swathed in bunting, flags and streamers before erupting into one long street fair that culminates in a massive parade on the saint's day (which also happens to coincide with the year's best market). Throughout the week the town becomes a rowdy riot of copious drinking, colourful costumes, grotesque masks, marimba music, energetic dancing and loud fireworks.

Here, too, it is possible to witness the amazing *palo volador* (flying pole) ritual in front of the white-painted church, where two acrobats spin impressively from ropes fastened to their ankles as they spiral outwards and downwards from a tall pine pole that has been consecrated as a continuing tribute to the Mayan *yaxche* (tree of life). Other highlights include another historic tradition – the Baile de la Conquista (Dance of the Conquest) in which masked dancers portray the invading Spanish conquistadors who arrived back in the 16th century. The whole extravaganza might have been staged for tourists, but isn't – instead representing the soul of Guatemala.

WHEN:
December
WHERE:
Chichicastenango (Chichi)
BEST FOR:
A unique blend of Mayan and Christian traditions
YOU SHOULD KNOW:
Before swinging into the Fiesta de Santo Tomás, the locals (along with the rest of the country) warm up on December 7 with the Quema del Diablo (Burning of the Devil).

Two acrobats spin on ropes in front of the church.

251

Isla del Sol

WHEN TO GO:
October to March, when the
days are warmer. Nights are
always cold.
HOW TO GET THERE:
By the principal ferry boat,
via several of Titicaca's
islands, to/from Puno (Peru)
from/to Guiaqui (Bolivia).
Backpackers can reach the
small Bolivian lakeside
village of Copacabana by
bus or car, then take an
open boat for the 1-hour
ride to Isla del Sol.
HIGHLIGHTS:
The settlement of
Challapampa, set among
Inca ruins in the 'V' of two
beaches narrowing into an
isthmus at the island's
northern tip.
Jacques Cousteau used a
mini-submarine to search
the offshore area for the
two-ton gold chain of Inca
Huascar, part of the
legendary Inca treasure
sunk in Titicaca when the
Spanish reached Cuzco.
The Bolivian 'beach town' of
Copacabana, site of the
Fiesta de la Virgen de la
Candelaria ('The Dark Virgin
of the Lake'), carved by Inca
Tito Yupanqui in 1592.

The biggest lake in South America, and the highest
navigable lake in the world, lies at 3,810 m (12,507 ft),
its 196 km (122 mi) length spanning the Andean
border between Peru and Bolivia. Lake Titicaca is the
cradle of Inca civilization – and Isla del Sol is the
Incas' holiest site. Here, Inti's (the Sun God's)
children, Manco Tupac and Mama Ocllo, burst from a
prominent sandstone crag called Titikala (the Sacred
Rock), banishing darkness and
bathing the world in the brilliance of
the re-born Sun. The Incas built a
temple on the rock, later expanded
by the 10th Inca Tupac, Inca
Yupanqui. He also built a convent
for the *mamaconas* (chosen
women) and a *tambo* (inn) for
visiting pilgrims – these are
among 180, mainly Inca, ruins on
the island. But the excavations at
Ch'uxuqulla, above the small Bay of
Challa, also show that Isla del Sol
had been a sacred place for at least
5,000 years before the Incas.

Even today, most things about
Lake Titicaca are at odds with the
modern, technological and political
world. The Aymara people who farm
Isla del Sol grow barley, quinoa
wheat, potatoes and maize on the
stepped terraces hacked into every
available surface of the harsh, rocky
terrain – just as their ancestors did
for millennia, while the Incas came
and went from power. Today, the
island is part of Bolivia, but power
and ownership simply don't matter

*A hiker stands on a
high point of Isla del Sol
overlooking Lake
Titicaca.*

when you are actually there. It's the resident Aymara who guard the spiritual continuum of the place. Their fishing, fields and alpaca herds allow no development of conventional tourist amenities or roads (though local families will happily rent you a cabin or room), and the way of life is utterly indifferent to visitors who pace and race. Coming from cities, take the time to pause and drink in the harsh geography, made beautiful by an innate and transcendent sense of peace.

YOU SHOULD KNOW:
The Aymara and Quechua of Lake Titicaca, and of Isla del Sol in particular, drive hard bargains in their dealings with the urban world of their visitors – but they are not of that world; and we trespass on their sacred sites.

Crowds gather at Sunset Dune.

Jericoacoara

Jericoacoara, a former fishing village in the north-east of Brazil, in the state of Ceará and close to the equator, was until recently an isolated area with little contact with modern civilization and no modern amenities like electricity, telephones, roads, television or even newspapers, and with an economy based on bartering fish for goods.

The government declared this extraordinarily beautiful place an Environmental Protection Area in 1994, and it has finally been reached by tourism, but its peaceful and unhurried atmosphere and its pristine natural environment are carefully maintained. To this end, hunting and building paved roads are forbidden, as is anything that might cause pollution. No buildings may be constructed outside the village, and all new homes must conform to the traditional architectural style. The number of tourists is limited by the number of amenities here and, despite the numbers of visitors who would like to travel to this paradise, no new hotels can be built.

A variety of different types of scenery and activities are available to entertain you at Jericoacoara, and the beach here has been voted as one of the ten most beautiful in the world. One of the best known attractions is the Arched Rock, a huge natural gate of stone sculpted by the waves over thousands of years. It is situated in the Rocky Region, an area which stretches along more than 2 km (1.2 mi) of coastline from Malhada Beach. It is just one of a seemingly endless sea of weirdly-shaped rocks, and caves that can be explored if accompanied by a guide. Make sure that you keep an eye on the tides, as this unique landscape is only accessible when the tide is out.

What makes Jericoacoara almost uniquely beautiful is that it is almost surrounded by sea, so it is possible to watch sunrise, sunset, moonrise and moonset over the blue waters. A tradition has sprung up for visitors to watch sunset from Sunset Dune to the west of the village. The lighthouse is the best place to observe sunrise and moonrise.

After sunset, locals demonstrate the ancient art of Capoeira by torchlight, a combination of fighting and dancing that was brought to South America by African slaves. A walk to the west of Sunset Dune brings you to an area called the Moving Sand Dunes, which are gradually encroaching on farmland. Another 5 km (3 mi) stroll takes you first to the isolated village of Mangue Seco, which stands by a freshwater lake, and then on to Guriu, a traditional fishing community which is so far virtually untouched by tourism.

WHEN TO GO:
Between 15 June and 30 July do not miss the sunset at Arched Rock. This is the only time of the year that the sun sets in the right place.
NAME:
From the tupi-guarani language: *yuruco* (hole) plus *cuara* (turtle), meaning 'hole of the turtles', as Jericoacoara is a beach where turtles come to make holes in which to lay their eggs.

Boca Juniors v River Plate

WHEN:
The match date varies within Argentina's soccer season (two round-robin competitions each calendar year).
WHERE:
Alberto J. Armando Stadium (better known as La Bombonera), Buenos Aires
BEST FOR:
Awesome sporting passion
YOU SHOULD KNOW:
The return derby at River Plate's Monumental de Nunez stadium is an even grander occasion, with over 75,000 fans present – but it somehow lacks the raw excitement of the match at Boca's more intimate ground.

At least half of Argentina's soccer fans support one of the capital's leading football teams – Boca Juniors and River Plate. These deadly rivals have been doing battle on (and sometimes off) the pitch for over 70 years and the annual derby match between the two clubs at Boca's extraordinary La Bombonera (Chocolate Box) ground is one of the world's great sporting occasions – a football match like no other.

The excitement as El Superclasico looms grips the country for days, given added spice by what each team represents. Both were founded in the deprived La Boca dockland area of Buenos Aires, but whilst Juniors stayed true to their humble roots River Plate moved to the smart Nuñez district in the 1930s. So now there's nothing fans of the 'people's team' like better than putting one over on the 'millionaires', as social class and money ignite volatile emotions.

The atmosphere within the ground has to be experienced to be believed, as anyone who has ever bought, begged or stolen a ticket will testify. Some 60,000 *barras bravas* (fanatical fans) occupy towering tiers of moving colour – blue and yellow for Boca, red and white for River. Banners wave, streamers stream, fireworks explode, dancers dance,

spectators surge and there's a wall of deafening noise as hard-core fans scream tribal chants and roar hysterically as the on-pitch contest unfolds.

The 'people's team' have an edge over 'the millionaires' – it's close, but Boca have won more of these epic contests. Passions always run high – Boca fans accuse their River counterparts of being *gallinas* (scared chickens) whilst River fans retort by calling Boca supporters *los puercos* (smelly pigs). Be warned – things sometimes get out of hand at El Superclasico time, with bitter rivalry spilling over into violence.

Ticker tape and streamers welcome the players on to the pitch.

ALTERNATIVE
ESCAPES

Stockholm Archipelago

WHEN TO GO:
Mid May to early September
HOW TO GET THERE:
From Stockholm, take scheduled or charter boats from outside the Grand Hotel; or get a boat pass from Waxholmsbolaget boat company, which enables you to travel anywhere in their timetable; or rent your own boat.
HIGHLIGHTS:
Dalarö Schweizerdalen, – beautiful white beaches.
Dalarö – 15th century church.
Utö – 200-year-old windmill with amazing view over the archipelago.
Kymmendö – a privately owned island where daytrippers are welcome to stroll through the fields and woods and see the cabin where August Strindberg stayed for seven summers.
Sandhamn Pine forest – a beautiful place for walks.
YOU SHOULD KNOW:
By far the best way to explore the Stockholm archipelago is in your own boat – to live out a Robinson Crusoe dream. Many of the islands are uninhabited and Swedish Public Rights of Access permit you to land almost anywhere and pitch a tent.

Sunset, peace and tranquility!

NEXT: Cottages in the archipelago

The Skärgården (skerry garden) stretches 60 km (40 mi) seawards from the city of Stockholm running some 150 km (95 mi) from north to south. It is an amazing labyrinth of some 24,000 forested granite islands, many of them less than 100 m (300 ft) apart. In the evening light especially, this maze of pine-covered rock floating in the sea is heartbreakingly beautiful. Here you can sail for miles, weaving your way past empty forested shores without seeing a soul. For hundreds of years the islands were sparsely populated by seafarers. Only in the 19th century did they start to become fashionable as a weekend retreat for wealthy Stockholmers.

Today, although the central archipelago is virtually a suburb of Stockholm, there are still some outstandingly beautiful places to visit.

The outermost island of Sandhamn is renowned for its splendid 18th and 19th century architecture, natural landscapes, and wonderful beaches; and Grinda, one of the tiny inner islands, is a famously romantic place for an overnight stay.

In the southern part of the archipelago, Dalarö is an old customs island with a picturesque charm; the surrounding islands are brilliant for camping and kayaking. Utö, one of the outermost islands, has superb swimming while Nåttarö is noted for its fauna, fishing and pretty country lanes. Nynäshamn is a bustling port with a charming harbour from where you catch the island-hopping ferry.

To the north, Tjockö is the main island of an archipelago of about 350 islands that have a long history as a base for piracy and smuggling. Arholma, the northernmost island of the Skärgården, has a charming old fishing village and amazing views.

Although it is one of the world's largest archipelagos, the Skärgården is relatively unknown outside Sweden. Its hauntingly beautiful atmosphere, an almost spiritual quality, is an extraordinary experience.

Bergen to Kirkenes

Large cruise ships ply the 2,000-km (1,250-mi) voyage between Bergen and Kirkenes, but for sheer intimacy it's difficult to beat the more informal service offered by the 'postal' ships that serve

HOW:
By postal boat
WHEN TO GO:
Year round
TIME IT TAKES:
Six or seven days one-way
HIGHLIGHTS:
The Lofoten Islands
The Sor-Varanger Museum
in Kirkenes
Bergen – full of Hanseatic
history
The lovely town of Bodø
YOU SHOULD KNOW:
Whilst the main purpose of
these vessels is to provide
supplies to far-flung
communities, the operators
do cater well for the tourist
trade. The vessels alternate
between day-time and
night-time deliveries, so that
anyone taking a round trip
will miss nothing.

NEXT: Fjaerlandsfjord

*View of Bodø from the
Coastal Express*

outlying Norwegian coastal communities. This odyssey takes you around Norway's breathtakingly beautiful fjord coastline, stopping over thirty times and showing you a side of Norway inaccessible by any other means of transport.

The journey begins in Bergen, a harbour town

founded by the Vikings almost a millennium ago, when it quickly became a vital hub, handling trade between Northern Europe and the British Isles.

As you leave the port, the splendid 14th-century gabled buildings of the seafront slowly dwindle to nothing and your eyes are drawn to the wonderfully rugged coastline. Along the way you will see glorious fjords, precipitous mountains and quaint fishing villages before crossing the Arctic Circle. Here, as you approach the North Cape, you will experience the midnight sun in the summer. Winter offers the chance to see the Northern Lights – the ultimate light show.

For much of the journey all eyes are fixed on the starboard side, where snow-capped mountains and fjords abound. This is until the vessel meanders between the Lofoten Islands whose stark, craggy beauty hits you from both sides. The trip gives you a true appreciation of this beautiful country and how most of its population clings to the coast. When you cross the Arctic Circle the population becomes more thinly spread and the scenery ever more dramatic. The awe-inspiring Laksefjorden and Tanafjorden lie ahead, before the vessel reaches its final destination, the sheltered port of Kirkenes.

Beautiful Geirangerfjord

Black Rock Cottage, Rannoch Moor

Glasgow to Mallaig

HOW:
By train

WHEN TO GO:
May to October (dour winter weather often obscures the scenery!)

TIME IT TAKES:
About five hours (Glasgow-Mallaig), of which the super-scenic Fort William to Mallaig leg takes 80 minutes.

HIGHLIGHTS:
Britain's only railway show shed, at Cruach Cutting shortly before the WHL's high point at Corrous Summit on vast Rannoch Moor.

At Banervie, where the WHL meets the Caledonian Canal – the amazing series of canal locks known as Neptune's Staircase.

Crossing the world-famous 21-arch Glenfinnan Viaduct in its truly spectacular setting.

Scotland's West Highland Line is a mighty fine line, especially for lovers of dramatic scenery. The WHL begins at Glasgow's Queen Street Station and takes a while to get going scenically – trundling through suburbs, Dumbarton and Helensburgh before turning north for Garelochhead. It gets up to landscape speed as it passes along the northwestern shore of Loch Lomond and reaches Crianlarich, where a western branch goes to Oban while the northern branch crosses wild Rannoch Moor before arriving at Fort William.

There beginneth one of the world's great scenic railway journeys, starting near Britain's highest mountain (Ben Nevis), crossing Britain's longest inland waterway (Caledonian Canal), visiting Britain's most westerly mainland station (Arisaig), passing Britain's deepest freshwater loch (Loch Morar), Scotland's whitest beach (Morar) and arriving at Europe's deepest sea loch (Loch Nevis). Nothing done by halves around these parts, then!

The train follows the rugged coastline, passing through many tunnels and small stations before reaching Mallaig, 265 km (165 mi) from Glasgow. You don't have to stop there – ferries link Mallaig to the Kyle of Lochalsh, Armadale, the Small Isles and the Isle of Skye. It's easy to turn a memorable Highlands journey into an unforgettable Highlands and Islands expedition.

It is also possible to marry the romance of steam with that overdose of magnificent Highland scenery, by taking a trip from Fort William to Mallaig and back on The Jacobite, a special service that runs on weekdays between mid-May and mid-October, with added weekend services in July and August. This not only offers the Highland sights, but also the evocative sound of steam...plus a leisurely stop at Glenfinnan where Bonnie Prince Charlie raised his standard in 1745 and time to explore the thriving fishing community of Mallaig.

The view from Arisaig Station on a clear day – spot the Small Isles of Rum, Eigg, Muck and Canna, plus the southern tip of Skye.
YOU SHOULD KNOW:
This trip was voted top railway journey in the world by *Wanderlust* magazine in 2009.

The silver sands of the Morar Peninsula

Polo World Cup on Snow

WHEN:
The last weekend in January
WHERE:
The lake, St Moritz
BEST FOR:
Dangerous sports, jet-set culture
YOU SHOULD KNOW:
Each of the four-man teams at the Polo World Cup on Snow carries a combined handicap in the range of 20 to 22 goals. According to the sport's stringent handicapping procedures, that's super-World Class.

The pitch is smaller but the surface is thrillingly different. Polo, one of the roughest and toughest sports on Earth, becomes a triumph of optimism over danger on snow. Only the very best even contemplate playing, and they like their skills to be matched to a location and circumstances worthy of their prowess. The Polo World Cup on Snow guarantees them the quality adventures they crave.

St Moritz and polo are both synonymous with glamour. The Engadine Valley in eastern Switzerland is famously beautiful in all seasons. Polo was first played here (informally) around 1897 by British subalterns looking for new excitement after founding the Cresta Run (in 1885).

The playground of the rich and famous for more than a century, St Moritz is in some ways more exclusive than ever – and polo is necessarily so, because players must invest fortunes to maintain their strings of ponies.

The World Cup on Snow allows only five ponies to each player for the four-chukka matches (instead of ten, for six chukkas); but the acclimatized ponies have studded shoes and special plastic 'over-bootees' against the ice and cold. Matches are fast, furious, and astonishingly graceful. Instead of the usual thunder on turf, you hear and see more acutely in the sharp air – the whinnied, snorting breath and creaking leather, and the swirling pillars of mist wherever players and ponies tangle in the cold. The razmatazz of parties during the tournament creates much the same impression.

Polo has been called the sport of kings, emperors and princes. It is, but the old-world charm of St Moritz makes the rarified social whirl of this competition feel inclusive to all comers. All you need to join in is a taste for madcap exhilaration, a pair of sunglasses for the evening, and a glass of champagne.

Polo players from Team Maybach (in cream) fight for the ball with players from Team Cartier (in red).

Burano

One of the few islands in the Venetian lagoon with sufficient character to emerge from the shadow of its illustrious neighbour, Burano lies 7 km (4 mi) north of Venice. It was settled by people from the Altino region on the mainland, escaping from the carnage of barbarian invasion in the 5-6th centuries. Like Venice, the flimsy wattle-and-daub houses were gradually replaced by stone houses for the fishing community that evolved here; and the tradition of brightly-painted houses for which it is now famous grew with the community.

Burano's isolation was reinforced by Venice's power: the Doges used it as a dumping-ground for victims of plague, malaria and madness. It became, and still is, self-sufficient, with a strong sense of workaday identity that makes it an authentic link in the fabric of Venetian social history. It has no airs or graces, and its ambience is the opposite of that inspired by the grandeur of the Grand Canal. It contains no major 'sights', and there's no space to facilitate a tourist industry, though the Buranese welcome visitors.

Burano is world-famous for its lace. Lacemaking developed over the centuries in the nimble fingers of the fishermen's wives, waiting for the boats to return, and from the 16th century to the end of the Venetian Republic in 1797 it enjoyed royal patronage. It was revived in the desperate winter of 1872, when ice prevented fishing, and Burano faced starvation. The ancient patterns and the delicacy of execution were immediately successful; but now there are no new apprentices to learn, and 'Burano' lace on sale is invariably machine made and imported. Otherwise, Burano is physically unchanged, except for the covering of one canal to make its only piazza. If Venice demands a series of superlatives, Burano is superlatively ordinary – and that is its beauty.

WHEN TO GO:
Year-round. The sound of lapping water, and the colours of the houses reflected in the canals are just as striking in winter mists as in the intensity of the sun.

HOW TO GET THERE:
By vaporetto (water-bus) No. LN (Laguna Norte) from the Fondamenta Nuove on Venice's north shore; or water-taxi from Marco Polo airport.

HIGHLIGHTS:
The impressive tilt of the 53 m (170 ft) high Campanile Storto ('Drunken Tower'), built in Renaissance style in the 17th century and restored with neo-classical elements between 1703-14.

The wonderful paintwork – amazing even by Burano's rainbow standard – of Casa Bepi Sua, the archetype of Buranese buildings.

Tiepolo's *Crucifixion*, painted in 1725, in the Chiesa di San Martino Vescovo.

The Museo del Merletto, the lacemaking museum of masterpieces including wedding dresses and parasols, some as old as the 15th century.

YOU SHOULD KNOW:
Philippe Starck, the interior designer known for his minimalist work, owns three houses on Burano.

Roses complement the intensely coloured house facade.

NEXT: A typical Burano 'street'

Naadam

WHEN:
July
WHERE:
Ulaanbaatar
BEST FOR:
Traditional sports and
national costumes
YOU SHOULD KNOW:
Although the biggest and
best Naadam is held in
Ulaanbaatar, small ones are
held all over Mongolia and
Buryatia.

The midsummer Naadam sports festival dates from
Mongolia's 12th century glory days under Genghis
Khan, when a man was measured by his prowess in
martial arts – the 'three manly games' of wrestling,
horse-racing and archery. More recently, under the
thumb of both Soviet Russia and China, the Mongolian
people suffered severe hardship, and the Naadam
sports have enormous significance in the public
consciousness as a ritual reminder of the country's
ancient heritage and successful bid for independence.

In the capital, Ulaanbaatar,
Naadam kicks off at the central
Sukhbaatar Square with a
spectacular parade of athletes,
monks, musicians and splendid-
looking mounted men dressed
and armed as Mogul warriors.
The games are held at the city's
main sports stadium, which at
Naadam looks more like a
fairground, bedecked with
coloured banners and souvenir
stalls while touts and food
vendors mill around amongst the
thousands of spectators plying
them with endless supplies of
the national diet – fermented
mare's milk and meat pancakes.

Popular as horse-racing and
archery are, it is the wrestling
that really gets the crowd going.
The passion it stirs is
comparable to soccer fever in
the West and there is an
atmosphere of febrile
anticipation when the burly

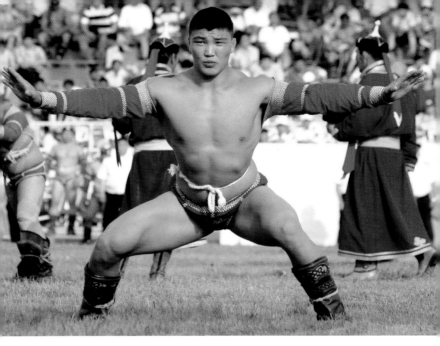

bare-chested wrestlers, wearing clumping great boots, tiny shorts and brightly coloured, tight little embroidered silk jackets, make their appearance. Before each fight the wrestlers perform an 'eagle dance' – an almost incongruously graceful, balletic movement with arms outstretched like wings. There are no weight divisions, no time limits and, apparently, few rules. The loser is the first to fall. Each wrestler has a *zasuul*, a personal sidekick who acts as protector and referee, chanting encouragement, and who, if his man wins, sings a victory song. You won't see a sports event like this anywhere else in the world.

A wrestler in traditional attire performs the eagle dance.

A child competes in a 23 km (14 mi) horserace – for children aged four to thirteen.

Pongal in Tamil Nadu

WHEN:
Mid-January – the auspicious date is calculated by the solar calendar and does not vary much.
WHERE:
State-wide in Tamil Nadu
BEST FOR:
Rice pudding and decorated cows
YOU SHOULD KNOW:
Kolams are seen outside homes and temples in Tamil Nadu all year. Coloured rice flour is carefully applied in intricate floral and geometric designs, inviting good fortune into the house. Their absence may indicate misfortune. The rice flour becomes food for ants and other small creatures, a mark of respect for life.

In Tamil Nadu, a state of towering temples, cool green hills and fertile farmland, the four-day harvest festival, Pongal, is a joyful time. Each day has its own rituals. Bhogi Pongal is a day of renewal when old cooking utensils are thrown out and discarded items are burnt on communal bonfires to symbolize a new beginning. A first harvest of rice, turmeric and sugarcane, cut using sickles consecrated with sandalwood paste, is brought in from the fields.

Surya Pongal is a day of rejoicing because the granaries are full, the sun shines and birds sing in blossoming trees. Surya, the sun god, is worshipped, then *pongal* (a dish of rice, sugar and milk) is cooked outside in streets decorated with flowers and rice-flour patterns – *kolams* – marked out by the women. To symbolize prosperity, the *pongal* is allowed to boil over, prompting happy cries of '*Pongal-o Pongal!*'

Maatu Pongal is a day for honouring the cattle. Washed and garlanded with wheatsheaves and flowers, horns painted and festooned with bells, the herds are led around the villages to receive homage. The animals are bowed to, touched respectfully on head and feet, and given a food offering of *pongal*. Although a dangerous sort of bull fight takes place in some villages, the last day – Kaanum Pongal – is

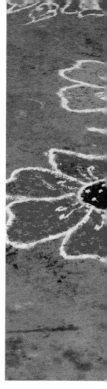

essentially a day for family visits and games.

This traditional rural festival is a particularly
cheerful one, when country people welcome the sun
and give thanks to God, earth and their cattle. Visitors
are welcomed and the tourist office in Madurai (a city
surrounded by rich agricultural countryside) provides
information and can arrange visits to nearby villages
where Pongal is celebrated traditionally and
enthusiastically.

*A traditional kolam is
painted on the street
and decorated with
flowers.*

*NEXT: The bull
takes aim!*

Ko Lanta Yai

WHEN TO GO:
November to March to
avoid the monsoon.
HOW TO GET THERE:
By ferry from the mainland,
Phuket or Ko Phi Phi
HIGHLIGHTS:
Ban Sangka-U, a traditional
Muslim fishing village.
Tham Mai Kaew, a series of
limestone caverns.
A boat trip to Ko Rok Nok
and Ko Rok Nai.
A night on tiny Ko Bubu.
YOU SHOULD KNOW:
Ko Lanta Yai escaped
relatively lightly from the
2004 tsunami, losing eleven
people. Tourists on the
island at the time set about
helping with the clean up,
and most businesses were
fully operational within just
a few days.

Situated off the coast of south-west Thailand, between the mainland and the Phi Phi islands, is another, less well-known archipelago, Ko Lanta. Made up of 52 islands, only 12 are inhabited, of which only three are easily accessible. Of these, Ko Lanta Yai is the largest, at 30 km (19 mi) long by 6 km (4 mi) wide. There are two main towns – Ban Sala Dan on the northern tip and Ban Ko Lanta, the district capital, in the east. This has bars, restaurants and shops, but remains a laid back, friendly place. Situated around the coast are several other villages and small resorts linked by a cement road.

Some of the archipelago is part of a National Marine Park; however Ko Lanta Yai is only partially protected, as much of the island belongs to the Chao Naam (sea gypsies) who settled here long ago. Fishing and tourism are mainstays of the economy and in the hilly interior, rubber trees, cashews and bananas are grown. Towards the south, pockets of forest still exist, though not for long if the developers have their way. For now, though, tourism is still less developed than it might be.

Visitors come for sun and sea, and the best beaches run all the way down the west coast of the island, virtually uninterrupted. Offshore there are coral reefs to marvel at and there is good diving just a boat ride away. The atmosphere on Ko Lanta Yai is less frenetic than that of Ko Phi Phi or Phuket, and development is slower. The joys of this place are simple – long walks on the beach, lazy days spent swimming, eating delicious seafood, reading, or just snoozing the day away in a comfortable hammock.

*A long-tail boat moored
at a beach.*

Fès – Fez el Bali

Fès is the 'symbolic heart' of Morocco – its intellectual, historical and spiritual capital. As you wander through its labyrinthine shady streets, exotic smells of mint and spices waft through the air,

dappled light falls on the whitewashed, crumbling grandeur of the old city and you can feel the tangible mystery and intrigue of this, the oldest of the four imperial cities.

Unlike many walled cities, Old Fès hasn't burst its banks, and its gates and walls remain intact. The

WHEN TO GO:
June to September on the Atlantic-Mediterranean coastline. March to June and September to December for the central plateau.
DON'T MISS:
Meknes, the Moroccan Versailles, surrounded by 40-km (25-mi) lime and earth walls.
WHAT TO BUY:
Leather goods, ceramics, spices and carpets.
WHAT TO EAT:
Harira, a hearty bean-based soup with vegetables and meat as well as Tagines, stewed vegetables, meat or fish cooked in earthernware cones, and cous cous. For the adventurous Pastilla de pigeon – pigeon meat, topped with scrambled eggs, then filo pastry, sugar and cinnamon.

The outdoor medina at Bab Chorfa Gate

population has expanded out of the city, flowing towards the south-west and arching towards the hillsides that stretch north and south of the new city. The towering Medersa Bou Inania, a theological college built in 1350, dominates the old city in the Fez River's fertile basin.

The medina of Fès el-Bali (Old Fès) is one of the largest living and working medieval cities in the world. Consisting of the 'traditional seven elements', mosques, medersas (Koranic schools), souks (markets), fondouks (lodging and trading houses), fountains, a hammam (steam bath) and a bakery, it is a bustling combination of city, museum and workshop that has changed very little with the passing of time. The streets are filled with artisans creating and selling their wares using traditional techniques. You can see baby-soft leathers being tanned, the sun glinting off copper pots as they are being soldered, brass plates being engraved, colourful ceramics and embroidery, cedar woodwork and carpets being hawked in hoarse voices that echo in the many courtyards. One of the experiences that cannot be missed is a stop into a Morrocan carpet shop. There

The entrance to the royal palace is a wonder to behold.

you will be plied with mint tea and shown hundreds of stunning, intricately woven rugs selling for a fraction of the price that you would pay in a department store for one of inferior quality. Some visitors may feel intimidated, but if you are looking for a quality carpet, and you enjoy bartering – this will be an unforgettable treat!

Elephants in Mole National Park drinking at a water hole.

Mole National Park Safari

Mole, an immense, remote tract of wooded savannah in northeast Ghana, is home to a huge range of animals (over 90 species including elephants, baboons, warthogs and antelope) and birds (300 species recorded, from tiny bee-eaters to vultures and eagles). However, its tourist potential is unrealized – 95 per

cent of its area is unvisited even by rangers, which has allowed regular poaching. The game-viewing circuit is limited to a few miles of poor roads around the southeast corner.

The area is best seen on foot and, unusually, most visitors arrive by public transport. The daily bus from Tamale (four to six hours west by dirt road) comes right into the Park. This is a crowded, dusty uncomfortable ride, with frequent breakdowns, but it is regarded as a memorable part of the Mole experience. Mole Motel, where the bus journey ends, is the only place to stay. The buildings are old and basic, the accommodation far from luxurious, the water supply erratic, but its situation, high on a steep escarpment above the savannah, is superb, affording views of the untouched wilderness landscape, the glorious sunsets and of two waterholes and the animals which gather there to drink.

Outside the hotel grounds, walkers must be accompanied by armed rangers (rifles protect against poachers, not big cats – lions have not been observed for some time). The hotel runs walking safaris in the early morning (cooler) and late afternoon, when more animals may be seen. These guided walks allow close-range observation of wildlife and can be tailored to the needs of the group.

HOW:
On foot
WHEN TO GO:
November to February
TIME IT TAKES:
Walks last three hours. Four days would allow for getting there and away and time to enjoy the Park.
HIGHLIGHTS:
The animals – particularly elephants bathing in the waterhole – they can be approached to within a few yards.
The birds – Mole has the longest bird checklist in Ghana. Even hardened birdwatchers are thrilled by the colourful, exotic and rare specimens.
The sounds of the savannah at night.
The staff canteen at the safari office serves traditional Ghanaian food.
YOU SHOULD KNOW:
Closed shoes are mandatory for guided walks. Tsetse flies can be a nuisance on the plain; carry netting to cover head and shoulders.

The Copper Canyon

HOW:
By train
DEPART:
Chihuahua
WHEN TO GO:
Best months: October to December, March and April
TIME IT TAKES:
About 16 hours (one way)
HIGHLIGHTS:
Chihuahua itself – a splendid historic city full of colonial treasures and monumental structures. The view from Divisadero, where the train obligingly stops for 20 minutes, so passengers can enjoy the sensational vista of three canyons (Tararecua, Urique and del Cobre).
YOU SHOULD KNOW:
If you should come across one of the frequent Tarahumara Indian celebrations, respect their privacy they are shy, proud people and it is polite to ask permission before taking photographs.

Anyone who has marvelled at the Grand Canyon has an even bigger treat in store south of the Mexican border. The awesome Copper Canyon complex in the Sierra Tarahumara consists of six linked canyons, collectively four times larger (and deeper) than their not-insignificant northern neighbour. The Parque Nacional Barranca del Cobre (Copper Canyon National Park) has been established to protect this remote but beautiful area in southwestern Chihuahua State, home to ultra-traditional Tarahumara Indians.

Happily, you don't have to hike this rugged country to experience Copper Canyon's incredible scenery, because you just have to catch a train and much (though not all) will be revealed. El Chepe, as the Chihuahua al Pacifico train is known, runs from the city of Chihuahua to Los Mochis near the Sea of Cortez, a distance of some 650 km (400 mi), traversing the principal canyon of Urique (North America's deepest). The line, completed in 1961, is a magnificent engineering feat, with 37 bridges and 86 tunnels. The quality of the scenery along the route is pretty good too – recognized by El Chepe's classification as 'one of the top ten most spectacular train trips in the world' in 2005. This accolade is justified – the extraordinary diversity of

this unique landscape ranges from snow-capped mountains to tropical forests in canyon bottoms.

There are four departures daily – two from each direction, one luxury and one standard – as the line is extensively used both by tourists and locals. But if you don't wish to take the full train journey, it is possible to stop off along the way to hike in and see attractions such as Candameñta Canyon's Piedra Volanda Falls (Mexico's highest) and the huge stone monolith known as Peña del Gigante. Guided tours are available to more remote destinations that El Chepe doesn't reach.

One of the 37 bridges El Chepe crosses on its journey.

NEXT: The Copper Canyon complex is four times larger (and deeper) than the Grand Canyon.

Tobago

WHEN TO GO:
Year-round. In mid-July, the 2-week Tobago Heritage Festival is an island-wide celebration of music, dance, food and song which you follow from village to village.

HOW TO GET THERE:
By air, from London, Atlanta and Miami; or via Port of Spain.

HIGHLIGHTS:
The tiered pools of the Argyle Waterfall, one of Tobago's loveliest rainforest cascades.

Fort King George (1779), commanding the heights over Scarborough, the capital, and its harbour.

Surfing the breaks at Mt Irvine beach; then meeting the locals at next-door Buccoo Beach for 'Sunday School', Tobago's hottest weekend event.

The 'Nylon Pool' – way out to sea, you jump out of the boat and walk waist-deep among the fish on the sandbar just below the surface. A truly weird sensation.

The spectacular coast drive to Speyside in the north, where offshore Goat Island is home to Tobago's famous manta rays.

Goat racing and crab racing - in villages, fields, or on the beach, at any time of day.

Tobago is the beautiful, reserved, soul-sister of jump-jiving Trinidad, its partner in the Republic. The contrast is awesome. Tobago is small. It has no major industry to impinge on its lush fertility. It has one main town, Scarborough, and dozens of hamlets and villages with names that reflect the Spanish, French, Dutch and English colonial powers which coveted it for centuries.

Outside the smallholdings of its sparse population, it's full of nature reserves harbouring wildlife otherwise found only on the South American mainland of which it was once part. At its highland heart, among the many waterfalls splashing down into idyllic bathing pools among the rocks and ferns, Tobago protects the oldest untouched tropical rainforest in the hemisphere. The 'rainy' season between June and December (short, sharp bursts, and a brilliant time to take a swim) freshens the landscape, which erupts into a natural carnival of colourful flowers; and this is matched underwater, where the myriad flashing shoals play lethal hide-and-seek among the cup coral in the canyons and deep caves where barracuda, dolphin and manta rays cruise. You can dig for chip-chip (a kind of shell fish) in the warm clear water of Manzanilla Bay, or hunt the big game fish like marlin, wahoo and yellow-fin tuna. You can have double fun in the knowledge that there's nothing in Tobago – in the water or on land – to kill you: no man-eating sharks, box jelly fish, bird-eating spiders, or poisonous snakes!

Undeveloped (no house, hotel or resort is allowed to build anything higher than a palm tree grows) and peaceful, Tobago does however know how to party. Carnival here is homespun, but just as colourful, rum-fuelled and demoniacally energetic as anywhere. What's more, you can practise every week throughout the year at the open air dance they call 'Sunday School'.

Swimmers in the Nylon Pool

Barrier Reef, Belize

WHAT IS IT:
The longest barrier reef in the Western Hemisphere

HOW TO GET THERE:
Fly to Belize City. Local flight or a 90-minute water taxi journey from Belize City to Ambergris Caye.

WHEN TO GO:
Temperature 24-30°C (75-86°F) all year. Best time of year is December to March. Rainy, hurricane season is May to November.

NEAREST TOWN:
San Pedro 58 km (36 mi) north of Belize City.

DON'T MISS:
The Great Blue Hole – one of the most astounding dive sites anywhere on Earth – a large almost perfectly circular limestone hole like a giant deep blue pupil in the turquoise sea. Inside, the water is 145 m (475 ft) deep and full of bizarre stalactite formations, growing ever more intricate the deeper you dive.

As you approach Belize from the air, you will see an unbroken line of white surf. A gigantic breakwater cleaves a 250 km (156 mi) long path through the sea, splitting the clear turquoise coastal waters from a dazzling royal blue ocean. This is the longest barrier reef in the Western Hemisphere. It is also one of the most diverse reef formations in the world. Apart from the Barrier Reef itself, there are fringing reefs along the coast and three atoll reefs, as well as sea grass beds and mangroves in the coastal wetlands,

The reef was designated a World Heritage Site in 1996.

A Queen Angelfish emerges from the reef.

altogether creating diverse ecosystems for an abundance of wildlife.

Divers witness a fabulous array of marine life – rainbow-tinged tropical fish, sea fans, mauve and purple sponges and golden red coral gardens. Around the atolls and outside the reef, where the seabed drops to depths of 3,000 m (10,000 ft), there are numerous big fish – stingrays, nurse and whale sharks, tuna, marlin. The most popular diving area is off the 40-km (25-mi) long Ambergris Caye, the largest of some 200 cayes that dot the coastline of Belize. The reef here is less than 2 km (1 mi) offshore and part of it is a conservation area with nesting grounds for three endangered species of sea turtle.

The Belize Reef is particularly species rich as it is one of the last places in the world with extensive areas of almost pristine reef, much of it as yet unexplored – so far around 350 fish and 65 coral species have been documented and it is expected that many more are waiting to be discovered. It is also a habitat for 200 kinds of bird, including hummingbirds, parakeets, blue herons and egrets.

YOU SHOULD KNOW:
Scientists estimate that over 40 per cent of the Barrier Reef has been damaged since 1998. Reef systems everywhere are under serious threat from pollution, coastal development, over-fishing and global warming.

Barranquilla Carnival

WHERE:
Barranquilla, Atálantico Department
WHEN:
Normally in February, occasionally in early March
BEST FOR:
Carnival excess as it's meant to be
YOU SHOULD KNOW:
Visitors to Barranquilla Carnival experience 'A Masterpiece of the Oral and Intangible Heritage of Humanity' (that's UNESCO's rather long-winded way of awarding Five Stars for Fun).

This is Colombia's spirited entry in the extensive lexicon of South American carnivals that explode to life in the run-up to the beginning of Lent on Ash Wednesday. And what an entry – for the Carnaval de Barranquilla is one of the world's largest fiestas. Although outdone by Rio Carnival in terms of sheer size, the Barranquilla Carnival is recognized as taking the top prize for being less commercial and more authentic than its Brazilian counterpart. Throughout four days of feast and frolic that build up with true Caribbean spontaneity to the final splurge on Fat Tuesday (Mardi Gras), the city is gridlocked as street dances, marching bands and masquerades bring traffic to a standstill.

Many types of Colombian music are performed, especially *cumbia*, and the atmospheric sound of drums and wind instruments is to be heard at every corner. Dances like the indigenous *mico y micas*, the African congo and Spanish *paloteo* are but three among many styles on display, whilst colourful costumes are everywhere – often adorning masked revellers who criss-cross the city engaging in *la burla* (poking fun). Larger-than-life puppets make stately progress with red-nose clowns capering about. Popular comedy performances maintain the carnival's oral traditions, whilst folkloric theatre and local choirs all add to the extraordinary atmosphere that infuses the city.

Highlights include the coronation of Rey Momo (Clown King) and Carnival Queen of Queens, a beauty pageant, Battle of Flowers (on Saturday) and a Grand Parade (on Sunday). Official processions use a rather run-down avenue in the port area, but the floats often proceed to the town centre where the locals really cut loose – spray foam, party poppers and flying flour are constant hazards as excitement reaches fever pitch. There is no argument – Barranquilla Carnival truly is the people's festival.

A female contestant in the Battle of Flowers, held on the first parade day.

COUNTRIES

PLACES

4Corners Images/SIME/Del Duca Patrizio 155.

Alamy/Dennis Campbell 281; /Chris Cheadle 173; /Danita Delimont/Greg Johnston 120-121; /Douglas Peebles Photography 293; /Ilja Dubovskis 83; /David Halbakken 168, 169; /Juergen Hasenkopf 23; /Nick Hughes 60-61; /Jam World Images 154; /John Warburton-Lee Photography 108-109; /Mike Kleinhenz 230-231; /Frans Lemmens 250; /LOOK Die Bildagentur der Fotografen GmbH/Hauke Dressler 84-85, Ingrid Firmhofer 254, Karl Johaentges 167; /Mayday 285; /Steve Mcinerny 233; /Holger Mette 107; /Michael DeFreitas North America 44; /Nordic Photos/Sigurgeir Jonasson 213, Kristjan Maack 80-81; /Peter Packer 94-95; /David Parker 93; /Photoshot Holdings, Ltd. 101; /Shane Pinder 119; /pixonnet.com/Bo Joelsson 139; /Robert Harding Picture Library Ltd./Colin Brynn 59, Roy Rainford 140; /Bert de Ruiter 165; /Bettina Strenske 214; /StockShot/Nick Yates 8-9, 10, 11; /Taka 152-153; /The Art Archive/Alfredo Dagli Orti 148; /Michael Treloar 209; /Yuri Varigin/Art Directors & TRIP 105; /David Wall 134-135.

Mick Briggs 258-259, 274, 276-277.

Corbis 53; /All Canada Photos/Sean White 46; /Theo Allofs 191, 192-193; /Adrian Arbib 160-161; /Atlantide Phototravel 222-223, 286-287; /Tom Bean 58; /Nathan Benn 116-117; /Richard Bickel 122; /Christophe Boisvieux 90-91; /Jan Butchofsky 125; /John Carnemolla 132-133; /Lee Cohen 12; /Diane Cook & Len Jenshel 57; /Ashley Cooper 74; /Design Pics/Paul Hobson 197, John Short 98-99; /Destinations 145, 147; /Ecoscene/Andrew Brown 141; /epa/Arno Balzarini 273, Jens Büttner 88-89, Vassil Donev 56, Jim Hollander 20-21, Cezaro de Luca 257, Ricardo Maldonado 301, Michael Reynolds 278, 279, Josu Santesteban 18-19; /Etsa/Malcolm Hanes 261; /Eye Ubiquitous/Paul Seheult 297; /fstop 241; /Gallo Images/Anthony Bannister 42, Diana Frances Jones 171; /GODONG/Michel Gounot 25; /Mike Grandmaison 110; /Judy Griesedieck 236; /Roger de la Harpe 172; /Blaine Harrington III 6 left, 294-295; /Jason Hawkes 271; /Hemis/Patrick Escudero 182, Patrick Frilet 126, Bertrand Gardel 184-185, Hervé Hughes 92, Camille Moirenc 102-103; /Jeremy Horner 78-79, 164; /Dave G. Houser 124, 210-211; /Rob Howard 35, 51, 177; /Dave Hunt 75; /Image Source 27, 266; /In Pictures/Paul Hackett 216-217, Barry Lewis 264-265, Christopher Pillitz 136-137; /JAI/Alan Copson 150-151, 237, Christian Kober 206-207, Julian Love 289, Max Milligan 290, John Warburton-Lee 187; /Johnér Images/Sven Halling 269, Jeppe Wikström 262-263; /Wolfgang Kaehler 181; /Catherine Karnow 201; /Kelly-Mooney Photography 115; /Bob Krist 228; /Frans Lanting 162; /Floris Leeuwenberg 7 left, 224; /Danny Lehman 54-55; /Jean-Pierre Lescourret 47; /Liu Liqun 33; /Gerd Ludwig 203, 204-205; /Joe McDonald 40; /John and Lisa Merrill 62-63; /David Muench 178-179; /Naturbild/Staffan Widstrand 36-37; /Richard T. Nowitz 104; /Ocean 174-175; /Charles O'Rear 225; /Matthieu Paley 100; /Paul C. Pet 24; /PictureNet 180; /Radius Images 2, 6 right, 68, 127, 128-129, 157, 159, 163; /Jose Fuste Raga 220; /Reuters/Andy Clark 176, Marcelo del Pozo 218-219; /Robert Harding World Imagery14-15, Adam Burton 16-17, Lee Frost 270, Gavin Hellier 186, Christian Kober 34, Graham Lawrence 22, Bruno Morandi 30-31, Louise Murray 195, Michael Runkel 28-29; /Galen Rowell 64-65, 70-71, 183; /Bob Sacha 112-113; /Paul A. Souders 52, 72-73, 196, 198-199; /Kim Sayer 142-143; /Science Faction/Frank Siteman 114, Stuart Westmorland 299, Norbert Wu 66; /Michel Setboun 32; /Richard Hamilton Smith 50; /Jon Sparks 97; /Specialist Stock/Michael S. Nolan 190; /Steve Parish Publishing 131; /Sygma/Frédéric Soltan 282-283; /Randy M. Ury 111; /Onne van der Wal 41; /Visuals Unlimited/Jim Wark 238-239; /Anthony John Wes 188-189; /Anthony West 253; /Michele Westmorland 77; /Stuart Westmorland 298; /Staffan Widstrand 7 right, 67; /Alison Wright 48; /Xinhua Press/Wang Ye 226-227; /Michael S. Yamashita 200.

Caren Davies 247, 248-249.

Mark Hill 86, 235, 242.

Lilian Levesque 245.

Volcanoes Safaris 38-39